TALKING TO UKRAINIANS

Далі присвячено народу України. Як би я не намагався пояснити свою точку зору якомога нейтральніше, я розумію, що те, що написано мною, буде піддано критиці. Хочу уточнити, що будь-який негативний коментар до Російської Федерації аж ніяк не є критикою росіян як народу.

The following is dedicated to the people of Ukraine. Much as I've tried to explain my point of view as neutrally as possible, I understand that what I wrote will be criticized. I want to clarify that any negative comment on the Russian Federation is by no means a criticism of Russians as a people.

Следующее посвящено народу Украины. Как бы я ни старался объяснить свою точку зрения как можно более нейтрально, я понимаю, что написанное мною, будет подвергнуто критике. Я хочу уточнить, что любой негативный комментарий к Российской Федерации ни в коем случае не является критикой россиян как народа

In loving memory of John Hryniuk.

CONTENTS

WHY DID I WRITE THIS?

For about six months, I lived and worked in Ukraine as part of the Government of Canada's assistance mission, as a response to the 2014 Maidan revolution. Consisting of a small detachment of military and foreign affairs officials, Canada's support to Ukraine is essentially based on economic support, limited military training of their armed forces and, as much as the geopolitical weight of Canada could mean to the international community, unapologetic (and public) support to Ukraine. With the ongoing warfighting in the eastern part of their state, Canada does what can to help Ukraine overcome yet another foreign intervention; a phenomenon sadly observable throughout their history. As I write this, Canada continues to support Ukraine in these difficult times.

All things being equal, Canada's commitment to Ukraine remains modest. While Canada did deploy hundreds of its soldiers as to help train of Ukrainian service personnel, from the onset there can be no secret: we did not, will not, and will never have the ability of the United States or of NATO to offer real solution. At best, Canada is a middle power that realistically stands no chance against the juggernauts of the Cold War. It's clear that both are hedging their bets on what comes next, and thankfully, Canada has already cast its small dice in favour of Ukraine.

A memorial to the war dead. There are thousands of such monuments throughout Ukraine; I have never seen one disrespected or poorly maintained.

To say that history been unkind to Ukraine would be the understatement of understatements. The Holodomor, World War Two, Soviet hegemony, Chernobyl, Maidan, all of these have been cast upon a largely agricultural state and are due to virtually no fault of their own. They have, some would say shockingly, survived most varieties of horror and have managed to stand against the probabilities of time, only to be faced with yet more issues that aren't of their doing.

Some will disagree with me when I say that Ukraine, as a now sovereign nation, has had it the worst of all former soviet bloc states. As I'll explain later, they are not part of the Russian Federation by both identity and culture; they don't think like them, they don't act like them. Yet, because they are neighbours and aren't insular, to the outsider (myself included), one would be initially tempted to dismiss those differences as artificial, at least until the uninformed foreigner takes the time to understand just what Ukraine consists of.

What follows is the written experience of one outsider that, I hope, was in country long enough to give justice to the things I saw, while trying to remain as neutral as possible. Vast amounts of literature exist on countries such as Poland or Germany: they have had economic successes, both have produced a Catholic Pope, and they have clear identities. For Ukraine, perhaps I write this because Canada might have a common theme on this point, our identity is not as clearly defined as our larger, more powerful neighbour. As a result, there isn't much that's written on Ukraine, even less so in an independent fashion, from Canada, and in English.

I wrote this book as a result of my experiences, perceptions, and understanding of how Ukrainians think and act. Why they act the way they do, of this I have no doubt, is based on the premise that the world that will continue to be unkind to them. While we all have an ability to make the best of a life that consists of mixed opportunities, in Ukraine whatever chances you have, if any, are sparse and highly sought out. In the following pages, my point isn't to remind Canadians of how lucky we are to live in a society where our quality of life and/or our identity isn't a constant, violent struggle. With that in mind, if I do make some Canadians more grateful, it would be a nice, unintended outcome.

For those who might think that the following pages contain information about the Ukrainian or Canadian military that might assist an adversary, you would be mistaken. I waited until an appropriate amount of time lapsed after leaving the Department of National Defence to write this book, and any comments that could even be interpreted as political statements are my own. That said, I am unapologetically patriotic and proud to be Canadian. I stand with any nation that seeks its own self-determination, sovereignty, and identity; with the understanding that this does not come at the cost of destroying another.

Finally, I realize that much of what I have written will, for many readers, come off as morose. I know that for most North Americans, the privilege that we live in is so taken for granted that, in a country sharing a similar culture to our own, surely, they too must be living better times than a generation or two beforehand. Let me be clear from the beginning: the situation that Ukraine finds itself in is not a charitable one, and what I witnessed, to use some metaphors, can't be sugar coated, spoon fed or artificially propped up. In other words, I will not do the very Canadian thing of only looking at the good while prettying up a situation: I will be honest, I will dignify the people I have talked to and will not tarnish the facts by wearing rose tinted glasses.

As a people, few have impressed me as much as Ukrainians. They are resilient in face of adversities that I know would be the downfall of most Canadians. They try hard, fail often, but always, always try again. I have rarely seen such determination and stubborn pride, summarized in their belief that they never quit, no matter what and no matter the degree of difficulty. This mentality, I strongly suspect, will continue to inspire for me for the rest of my days.

Leaving a grocery store near Lviv, an old man and what I'm assuming was his grandson were collecting money for the ongoing fighting in the eastern part of their country; mainly to go towards purchasing clothing and foodstuffs. Finding out that I was Canadian, his only comment to me in broken English is that he wished that he could continue to fight for his country, and thanked me for helping. I asked him how long he thinks the fighting will last, and he told me that he never expects it to finish; that it will go on like the history of Ukraine, through sacrifice.

In a country where struggle never stops, its people have adjusted to the idea that the control they have is to sacrifice, to keep going. From my time in Ukraine, it was obvious that people do not expect things to get better anytime soon; what they want is to never contribute to making it worse.

A VERY ROUGH HISTORY

Like all nations, Ukraine colours its understanding of the world based on its past. There are reasons, many in fact, as to why Ukrainians are suspicious of the intentions of others, deeply committed to their families, and respect religious institutions in a far more meaningful way than most of us in the Americas ever will. To be reductionist: there isn't much else, past their families and personal beliefs, that Ukrainians can look at for examples to follow.

To a Western mind, or should I say more accurately one from North America, the hardest part in understanding Ukrainians is to appreciate their suffering. Nobody in Canada or the United States can remember what it was like when we were living through invasion, oppression, or war from a foreign government on our own soil; these actions, depending on how we gauge them, ended centuries ago.

Past the monuments in Canada to either

Frontenac or Brock, or those in the United States that include Jefferson or Washington, wars of occupation on our home soil are in the distant past. The men and women that fought for their ideals are no longer with us, and we are left with a collective memory based largely on textbooks. For Ukraine, such memories are known not only to their parents; they are experience an ongoing reality of struggle, that I assure you, is very real.

To me, this understanding began when I first landed in Ukraine.

Past the obvious state of decay, the introduction was modest.

Lviv's international airport. A modern, towering set of structures that was built on the promise of a new world. Something that wasn't like the Soviet Union, something only Ukrainian; what that would look like nobody, if they're honest with themselves, knows for sure. That Ukraine hasn't existed since at least 1933.

Everything is built with metal and concrete slabs, made to look like polished marble. The customs people wear what appears to be the ridiculously large soviet hats and the women wear these odd, tall boots, making them look like cosmonauts or something, as they check your papers and examine them as if they're curing cancer. No, I'm not bringing weapons with me- yes, I'm here for work. Stamp ka-chink goes one of many ink clad metal seals on my passport, as her deep, curiously blue eyes scrutinize me for just one more second before she says next.

The interior of the airport is impeccable, and I don't know why I thought this immediately; they're trying too hard to look like Europe. Yes, in the geographic sense of the word, that Ukraine is part of Europe is fact. That said, that they are located somewhere between Russia and Poland is far more relevant: if they could change their geographic location, I have no doubt that it would be west of Poland, preferably past where you find most Czechs.

Any thoughts of modernity, if I could even call it as such, ends right after leaving the airport.

So that I could meet my new boss as soon as possible, two staff members picked me up at the airport. Destination: a small town/city called Starichy, maybe 45 minutes by car. Seeing what was probably the one non paler than pale tourist-looking guy, looking around for someone that had sign with my name on it (or the like), the drivers came up to me, said my last name, and I nodded. I was in no mood for conversation really, something about ten hours on a red eye and an obese man snoring his apnea away, six inches or less from my face, did not help my generalized mood.

Twenty seconds after you leave the airport grounds is when you start to see their country. Ukraine, even in the western segments, that is, the wealthier, less soviet parts of it is, in one word, poor. More accurately and in eight: when the Soviet Union left, nothing replaced it.

The roads were dissolving, the buses were of a sickly yellow colour that was clearly worn from the sun, nothing here looked new, modern, or even to a standard of basic use. Were any of this in Canada (and I fully realize, we are not in Canada), I have no doubt that it would all be condemned, or civil servants would, I might add rightly, strike to make their grievances heard.

Everyone looks the same, there are no immigrants to speak of. Nobody said to themselves in the third world that they should move to Ukraine to make a better life for their kids. No, what you have instead is a homogenous mass of seemingly well-dressed people living in buildings that, from my totally uninformed mind, look like they were built in the early sixties, with little investment since then.

It's sad. The hunchback old woman carrying her sack of whatever, slowly walking on a never-ending, perfectly straight street, all of them wearing a scarf to cover their heads. The children, none of them fat, all of them with slightly sunken eyes, looking at your car (and why the hell did they get a new rental, I mean could we stand out more?) and wondering what an alien you are, where you could possibly be from. At every red light more children notice your clean, jet-black four-wheel drive, pausing to stare at you not out of admiration, jealously or want. No, it's simply that you don't belong in this kind of scenery, and the question that's clearly warranted is who you are and what could you possibly be doing here.

Advertisements seem to be all about the West and the modern. Apple, Microsoft, trips to Paris, trips to London, all huge billboards with actors that are looking at you in stoic, barely half smiles that you can kind of make out if you look long enough. Stoicism: always present, never exaggerated, I would suspect that the average local, looking at a family album from the West would think that we're insane extraverts, smiling like we're possessed in every photo we have. Cool and calculated, only the young appear to have a thought about entertainment or laughter; the rest walk, never run, to their obligations.

Stopping for gas is the first thing I did, past sitting in a car to get the above-mentioned preview. Along the way, both staff get out of the car and do the most mundane of mundane, when another introduction came along.

The cost of gas? Same as in Canada. Average salary? About a twentieth.

What looked like a Lada from the early eighties pulled up at the other solitary pump, with what appeared to be a well-dressed man with an old timey Irish cap, giving a large wad of bills to the guy that pumps gas. While the pumping guy does his job, I'm stretching my legs outside of my black behemoth; I see in the back of this very small car what seems to be a mother, three young children, a father, followed by another adult in the front seat with a baby on her lap. All of them, as I step out of the large rental look at me with little subtility, children especially, and knew right away that I'm not from here.

Physically I might look, somewhat, the same as they do. Dressed well, I might even fit in somewhere in downtown Lviv or Kyiv. Yet those appearances are fleeting, they are imperfect, and they do not stand up to much scrutiny. The way you walk, the way that you look at others and until you figure out that sunglasses are a fashion statement in most of the world, not a device to shield you from the sun (read: throw them in the trash), you are easily identifiable.

The well-dressed man with the Irish cap looked at me exit the back seat, nodded very slightly, and put his wallet back into his pocket. To my mind, he was purposely looking away from me. A few days later I told this story to an interpreter: his view was that they probably saw me as an authority figure that had been bothered by some village idiot. As a result, the interpreter's theory is that the locals thought I had to leave my downtown palace to settle a score. Violently, I ask, or was it more of a bureaucratic shakedown.

It doesn't really matter, said the interpreter. The reason why those kids were probably looking at you a bit, and the well-dressed man didn't at all, is that, for them, power from the state or power from crime is the same thing: whoever has the most makes the rules. They know that they have no power, and that you walk out of a brand-new car, with what looked like two goons doing the menial is a controlling statement on your part, even if you didn't know it. They were at least nervous, maybe a little afraid, the second you stepped out of that back seat and looked in their direction.

This, in the smallest possible sense, is Ukraine. A land of people that are struggling through times more difficult than most Westerners will ever know, a people that are profoundly distrustful of others, and who could ever blame them. My preview of Ukraine made me realize what Canada would probably have looked like if it were absorbed into the Soviet Union, the mere happenstance of geography saving my country from most of what Ukraine continually deals with. A mix of sadness, admiration, looking at them on one hand as completely foreign to me, on the other eerily similar. In some very distant Eurocentric way of looking at life, still parsed by at least half a millennia of history, the common traits or hard work, family and honour were more present in Ukraine than I have generally found in Canada.

This brings me to how I should introduce you to Ukraine, at least from the historical standpoint. Thousands of years condensed into one chapter seems almost a joke to me- looking back to the beginning on the twentieth century seems more realistic. Yet, before I get into my conversations with Ukrainians, it seems only fair that I roughly, and meekly, draw the boldest of strokes and introduce you to their past.

Were you to go back to the era of the Tzars, just before the end of the First World War, what we now call Ukraine simply didn't exist. To the West, in cities like Lviv, this segment of Ukraine was part of the now dissolved Polish Empire. While less than 2% of locals now speak Polish, the legacy is still very apparent. I don't think I've ever seen more statues of Pope John Paul II; for that matter, most of the names of cities or towns remain Polish. Catholicism is very present and Russian, while commonly spoken, is certainly not the de jure language of most locals: that would be Ukrainian. The western part of Ukraine is considered, at least linguistically, as the heart of their civilization.

In terms of European countries, it is the second largest geographically, and due to its agricultural base, is often referred to as "the breadbasket of Europe." To the casual observer, one could think that Ukrainian is the most present language, yet in the eastern part of Ukraine, Russian is far more prevalent. This duality was not so much present as it was enforced: apart from the very isolated or, I say this as kindly as I can, irrelevant parts of Ukraine, people needed to speak Russian (and they still do) as to be part of the larger business diaspora.

As a modern country, Ukraine started to emerge once the Second Polish Empire dissolved and the Tzars were removed by the communists. In the 1920's, Ukraine vacillated from being under the de-facto control of either the Soviet Union or having de-jure sovereignty in certain regions, due chiefly to highly organized resistance movements. These groups did not last.

Stalin did not take kindly to the negative interpretations of others, and so, within a matter of weeks, he created an artificial famine as to choke Ukraine into submission. Thousands of communist henchmen effectively, and might I add brutally, removed virtually all food stores in Ukraine. There are sixteen nations on earth, mine included, that view this starvation campaign as a genocide. This barbarity is simply labelled the as the Holodomor.

The national monument to the victims of the Holodomor, located in downtown Kyiv.

As a state sponsored action, the Holodomor was one of the largest mass starvations in history, second only to that enacted in China by another communist dictator, Chairman Mao.[1] While we will never know the number of dead directly attributable to Stalin's butchers, the most conservative guess is that at least three million civilians perished, with some estimates as high as twelve. To contextualize just how many died, and again this is in using the most conservative numbers, at least one Ukrainian out of ten perished within a period of about nine months.

Immediately denied by the communists, any discussion of the Holodomor was quashed for decades on end. This means that with all their dead not yet buried, combined with Ukraine being forced to join the Soviet Union, the party line was that the Holodomor never happened. Of all the insanities that followed, one of the worst was how the very individuals that survived the Holodomor were denied the facts that they suffered through. It's worth repeating: people were effectively barred from even talking about their lived experiences. Should any have been so foolish as to talk about it, the Stalinists would have been delighted to sent them to a work camp, or worse.

And unfortunately, the Holodomor is just one segment of Ukraine's suffering.

Ukraine's involvement in the Second World War concluded to one of two options. Either maintain a semblance of a life under the Soviet jackboot or ally yourself to one that was German. For option number two, that meant being subservient to the Third Reich.

When Poland was invaded by both the Soviet Union and Germany,[2] two of the worlds largest armies invaded what was a much smaller, highly isolated country. Much as Poland fought valiantly, the odds of being able to stave off both the Third Reich and the USSR, at the same time no less, were essentially nil. After a few weeks of brutal combat, the Polish government had no choice but to capitulate, resulting in Germany annexing one half of Poland, the USSR the other. What this did, for the purposes of Ukraine, is that any remnant of the Polish Empire, to include mere cultural influence, was essentially dissolved. Ukraine was now under the solitary control of the soviets.

Less than two years later, Hitler invaded the Soviet Union and achieved an impressive (albeit short-lived) tactical success. At least initially, the Red Army was unable to even slow down the arrival of the Third Reich, and their sphere of control dissolved very quickly in most parts of Ukraine. From Poland, to Stalin, now Hitler, the idea of having another foreign state control the lives of Ukrainians was not new; what was, however, was the thought of removing the Soviets once and for all.

As a result of yet another occupier, Ukrainians had an opportunity to rid themselves of Stalinism and from the perspective of that time, becoming an ally (indeed a vasal), to the Third Reich was viewed as a completely acceptable option. From here, you have units such as the 14th Waffen Grenadier Division of the SS (1st Galician), a unit that remains a household name in Ukraine, simply referred as the Galician.

To this day, Ukraine celebrates this unit on an

annual basis; you can see their emblem at football matches throughout their country. At the Lychakivskiy Cemetery in Lviv, the Ukrainian army has the rough equivalent of an honour guard that stands post to a memorial to the Galician. To them, this unit is absolutely not seen as Nazi unit (even though it was); they view the Galician as an entity that fought off the Red Army as best they could, carrying the torch of violent descent from a generation ago towards the same adversary.

The Soviet Union did not look kindly towards rebellion. In a war that cost the lives of millions of Ukrainians, it first began with the Soviets, then the Nazis, to the eventual return of the USSR. Each time, over deaths that sometimes surpassed 100,000 per month, Ukraine suffered in front of two military juggernauts that viewed them, depending on the year, as traitors to their cause. In the end Hitler did lose and Stalin had every intention of making disloyal Ukrainians pay. Through the actions of one mainly one man, Pavlo Shandruk (his name is worth mentioning), did hundreds of thousands of Ukrainian soldiers manage to escape deportation, and almost certain death, should they have been transferred to the Soviet Union.

At the same time there was another group that fought valiantly with the Soviets against the Third Reich. For these Ukrainians, they fought with the Red Army throughout the Second World War, often outside of Ukraine, and there can be no question of their loyalty to both Moscow and their homeland. After all, over ten military Marshals and thousands of recipients of the Hero of The Soviet Union, USSR's most prestigious honour, were Ukrainian.

A compendium of thousands of pages could be written on Ukraine's involvement in the Second World War and no summary could ever give their sacrifice justice, much less mine. Over sixteen percent of the overall population of Ukraine died in this war: this number, as a ratio, is even larger that the deaths that occurred in what we now call the Russian Federation and was second highest within the Soviet Union.

After the defeat of Nazi Germany and for the next 45 years, Ukraine was an unquestioned part of the USSR. While rebellions in Poland and the Czech Republic were quashed from time to time, such actions within Ukraine were relatively modest- as far as we know. The de-facto language in most institutions, virtually all academic spheres, the press, international relations, and so on, was Russian.

I remember talking to an interpreter of a certain age that remembered what it was like to live in Kyiv in the early eighties. To his recollection, the only thing that was even remotely Ukrainian, media wise, was a children's cartoon program that was aired shortly before bedtimes. Past this, it was almost perceived as controversial to speak Ukrainian in public; Kyiv to them was never called as such, it was Kiev. University professors were either Russian, as in from Russia, or belonged to a group that was carefully vetted by Moscow.

From this interpreter's memories, it was clear to me that there was an obvious attempt on the part of the USSR to remove Ukrainian identity, culture, and language altogether. One of the questions I would often ask is where could you even live in Ukraine, if anywhere, and not speak Russian? For those that were aged 40 or above, they would tell me that if you wanted to be more than a farmer, a simple shopkeeper in a rural setting, or a manual labourer of sorts, there were no area where Russian was not their lingua franca.[3]

Only now, more than 30 years after the USSR dissolved, are you slowly starting to see university staff (especially those in positions of power) who are both culturally Ukrainian and owe nothing to Moscow. From a linguistic point of view, there's little doubt that Ukrainian is going through a revival, albeit slowly.

So homogenized was Ukraine, or so thought the USSR, that it held a large part of its nuclear arsenal.[4] How large? For a brief period after the collapse of the Soviet Union, Ukraine found itself as the worlds third largest nuclear power, and it came at a particularly bad time.

Communism breeds corruption, nepotism, and ineffective government. In the case of Ukraine, we are speaking of a several generations of communist thought. Essentially, this trail of thinking goes something like this, my thought being half borrowed from Orwell as to pen this poem:

We are all equal in the eyes of the Soviet state.
Until someone has more influence or power,
some becoming more equal than others,
in the perfect equality of our fates.

The result of mass induced communist thought was a nearly parasitic fascination with those in power- one of my colleagues best described this phenomenon as "Soviet Cynicism." This is the understanding that unless you're truly brilliant, without people that know of and speak highly of you, it's impossible for you to thrive. The state, master and commander of all things that matter, including your education, career, prospects in arts, sciences, and more, decides what you will do, when you will do it. With this understanding, the people at the top of the state apparatus become extremely popular, worshipped even, and in turn, nepotism, and a complete lack of transparency result in opportunities for the lucky few.

Explained another way: if you wanted to get ahead in Ukraine, you would be insane not to pander to the powerful. To that, I would add that you would be the idiot of idiots to think you're any smarter than the state, or that you could somehow control it. You want to get ahead? You will conform.

While this may seem bleak, even bleaker is when this becomes a generational problem. For Ukraine, there is no lived memory of what life was like before communist control: you would have had to be in your late eighties, maybe, to have childhood memories of such a life. Nobody knew of a better way to live, much less govern.

The problem with this mindset, barring the obvious corruption and the like, was historical timing. In the early nineties, what the West thought was the juggernaut that we would one day go to war with, what would probably end life on earth through World War Three, dissolved in a matter of months. I was too young to remember most of it, although those older than me were unanimous: nobody believed that the USSR was dissolving until the proof became unbearably damming. The flags were indeed coming down from a divided Berlin. Thousands were flooding the streets to the West, with the communist systems struggling in vain to maintain the illusions of collective East that never worked to begin with.

For most countries formerly part of the USSR, a partial list that includes Poland, Romania, the Czech Republic, Hungary, Lithuania, it did not take long for them to throw off their shackles. For most, they maintain a crystal-clear memory of what life was likely under communist control, and I would be shocked that they would ever consider returning to that supposed proletariat bliss.

Take Poland. In 1989, both Ukraine and Poland were of comparable size, population, and economy. By most standards, they were equally contaminated with communist mindsets, each had sluggish economies and their prospects for the future were dubious. Historically speaking, the twentieth century was a death struggle for Poland, and its prospects after the fall of the Soviet Union were about as good as any ex-vassal in Eastern Europe.

Yet, thirty years later, Poland has had outstanding success. Its economy has boomed, their stance on human rights, while imperfect, is certainly doing well; equality of women, transparency of government, the Polish nation is, by any metric, progressing. There are various reasons for this: I suspect Pope John Paul II being a symbol of anti-communist thought is partly responsible. Another could be the exposure to more Western European ways of business, those that would trickle in through a unified Germany. What I do know for sure is that hard work, dedication, and commitment are fundamental ingredients as to why the Polish have done well.

Ukraine was different. The 1990's were worse for Ukraine than the previous forty years combined, at least from an economic standpoint. Under communist rule everyone ate, if only badly, everyone had employment and the state, through all its problems, was able to provide for Ukrainians. With the USSR now dissolved, most economic relationships, military investment or scientific development that used to benefit Ukraine had effectively evaporated. The economic outcome of sudden sovereignty was so bad that its GDP, at the dawn of the 21st century, was about half of what it was in 1990. By contrast, the GDP of Poland, in the same timeframe, quintupled. For Ukraine, it seems that when Moscow left, so did the money.

These were not lean years; they were wretched. The hardships Ukraine faced were so bad that their level of absolute poverty, loosely defined as not being able to provide for essential needs, was assessed by the United Nations in 2001 be around 32%. These numbers are comparable to sub-Saharan African states and various third world countries, to include Haiti, had numbers that were better than Ukraine's.

I briefly mentioned earlier how Ukraine had become, by measure of the Soviet Union dissolving in short order, one of the largest nuclear powers on earth. With Ukraine having declared its independence in 1991, it now had enough nuclear weapons to lay waste to Europe in it's entirely, or perhaps just as realistically, the Russian Federation. Yet, in 1994, the Ukrainian government agreed to a deal brokered with the Russian Federation, one I suspect they bitterly regret.

The deal, contained in a document called the Budapest Memorandum on Security Assurances, was agreed to by most of the world's nuclear powers.

In sum, it guaranteed to various former vassal states of the USSR, Ukraine included, full autonomy in return for the denuclearization of their stockpiles. Ukraine agreed, with the understanding that the far larger behemoth that will always be its neighbor, now called the Russian Federation, swore that no interventions into their territory would ever occur. Did Ukraine agree to this as to ensure sovereignty on its territory, or maybe to appease the risk of nuclear war? Historians are divided.

Through the first decade of the 21st century, Ukraine did get better.[5] When looking at data from the World Bank and the United Nations, the most likely reason relates to debt limits, dissolving of public infrastructure, and the privatization that capped somewhere in the mid to late 1990's. After this, there was "some" development with independent industries that weren't state owned. Ukraine was learning how to work its own independent national economy, one that isn't communist. In contrast to other former soviet bloc states, there wasn't an Austria or a Germany as a neighbor and Ukraine stood struggling beside the Russian Federation, it too having great difficulties adjusting.

With this backdrop, we reach 2013/2014, a time barely old enough to be part of history, now called the Euromaidan. As I see it, this was the total collapse of a pro-Russian Federation government, ousted by a completely fed up people, and these actions would forever change Ukraine.

There's little doubt that the reason why Euromaidan happened is because of the power struggle between the European Union (i.e., the Western world), and the former overseer of Ukraine, the Russian Federation. In most events in history, there tends to be this shining example of why things are as bad as they are and how it got there; something about a symbol that essentially summarizes the mess that people find themselves in. For Zimbabwe, it would be inflation that requires a trillion-dollar bill. For Afghanistan, it would be the Taliban destroying thousand-year-old statues of the Buddha. For Ukraine, it would be the Mezhyhirya Residence, located near Kyiv.

It's as if an imperial palace met the most lavish wooden structure in the world, mated, and had a very fat baby. Starting with the windows that are hilariously out of proportion, the place looks absurd. The gardens look like they're from Versailles, the guest house is large enough to fit a family of 30, the "gazebo" looks like it was taken from the Acropolis. I'm not sure when the animals were brought to the grounds (think ostriches, noble looking deer, and colourful ducks), although an employee from the local zoo now feeds them. As the building had been used by high-ranking officials since the 1930's, some of them must have had vivid imaginations.

Just by looking at this thing, you would need a staff of 25 to maintain it. From 2009 to 2010, approximately 10 million USD was invested into this playground for upgrades. To add to the absurdity, what looks like a pirate-ship (or a barge) is on the property in its own miniature lake, commissioned less than 20 years ago. The boat's gold leaf finishing, marble carvings, and opulence that would make a Tzar blush includes a chandelier assessed by the newspaper Ukrayinska Pravda to be worth nearly $100,000 USD. The purpose of the barge? It's an office space for one person, transformable into a party room that can entertain hundreds.

As for the Mezhyhirya Residence proper, there is no way that I can sufficiently describe the interior. Somewhere between the exotic birds cheeping their rarely heard songs, the marble statues, medieval armour collections, Graeco-Roman facades of Olympians battling one another, passing through a giant building that has a grand total of two bedrooms, I have rarely seen such opulence. It looked like a mad billionaire decided to spend as much money as he could on the most expensive things he could find, and the result is simply decadent.

Since Maidan, the residence is now a tourist attraction and colloquially referred to as the Museum of Corruption; I can't think of a better nickname. If one wants to know, in a nutshell, what exactly caused Maidan to happen, all you need to do is visit this absurd monstrosity that was entirely, so far as we know, a playground for politicians and the super rich. At a time when Ukrainians were desperately struggling to survive, here stands a building that proves very well what went wrong in their country.

As he sat in that palace, right before Maidan, I wonder what Viktor Fedorovych Yanukovych, the fourth President of Ukraine, was thinking. You couldn't find a man that was more aligned with the intentions of the Russian Federation: he rejected a landmark agreement between Ukraine and the European Union that would have allowed for real economic partnership, known as the Ukraine-European Association Agreement. As an alternative, he chose to receive bailout money from the Russian Federation, and it was this decision that eventually led to his exile.

This is a man that stated the Holodomor wasn't a genocide and that it was unfair to blame Russia, even in a historical sense, for the deaths of millions of people. This is a man that praised Russian intelligence services, to include the GRU, as a positive force within Ukraine. A few months after getting elected, he signed a landmark deal with the Russian Federation to have their naval base in Crimea established for at least another 25 years; and it is a huge installation. Finally, despite having consistently claimed to be a Ukrainian patriot, he fled to Russia during the Euromaidan and was tried in absentia. Should he ever return, Yanukovych would be jailed for at least 13 years, essentially due to his gross mismanagement of the 2014 protests that resulted in civilian casualties.

The writing is on the wall in that the power structure that existed in Ukraine, circa 1991 to 2014, was either so corrupt or totally controlled by Moscow (or both?) that one can question what sovereignty it had. The tipping point did happen though, and the last straw from a furious, fed-up citizenry was seen for months on end in some of the most violent protests seen in Eastern Europe since the fall of the Berlin Wall.

The Russian Federation is not stupid: it knew that the man ousted was their own, and whomever would replace him would not be as allied. Seeing that Ukraine just might have gone the same way as Poland or the Czechoslovakia (amongst others), what became an incredibly amoral, pragmatic act unfolded in the eastern part of Ukraine. By April of 2014, just as Euromaidan was concluding into a change of elected officials, armed men within two of the poorest oblasts in Ukraine, I speak here of Luhansk and Donetsk,[6] violently overthrew provincial control.

What I will generously refer to as elections were called and the results, none of them recognized internationally by either mandate or process, resulted in a call to cede from Ukraine. In May of 2014, the so-called leader of Donetsk, whom I will not even dignify by naming, requested that Moscow incorporate his fiefdom into the Russian Federation. Remember Yanukovych? At around that time, exiled in Russia, he called for the Ukrainian government to remove their "mercenaries" from the ATO and respect the will of the Ukrainian people. To qualify his statements as absurd and hypocritical would be insufficient.

I could tell you about the convoys of Russian equipment brough into the ATO without permission from the Ukrainian government, that, when caught, the Russian Federation claimed they consisted only of medical supplies. I could tell you about the contradictory claims in that one day the Russian government claims having no military presence in the ATO, and on another saying they do. I could talk about the equipment that never existed in Ukrainian stockpiles, confiscated in the ATO and paraded in Kyiv as proof of Russian invasion, and, over the course of what you'll be reading, much of this will be discussed.

The guarantees and supposedly legally binding agreements signed over two decades ago, those that made it clear that the Russian Federation will never intervene in Ukrainian soil, in exchange for nuclear disbarment, are now all but openly accepted as a farce. It isn't in my nature to qualify my remarks so harshly; the facts simply do not allow for much in the way of a conciliatory tone.

Much has happened since Euromaidan. A new president was elected, then another. There have been various events that happened in the last twenty years that I have not discussed as my aim is to give a cursory overview; I'll suggest follow-on readings at the end. I do not mean to diminish Crimea, the Orange Revolution, Yulia Tymoshenko or the current president of Ukraine, Volodymyr Zelensky. All these individuals and events matter; it is simply that the rough overview of Ukraine can be discussed without them.

The following pages consist of my interactions with a people and a country between crossroads, and the values and ethics that, I believe, will be the salvation of Ukraine. To allow myself the first line of their national anthem: Ще не вмерла України ні слава, ні воля, or in English, the Glory and Freedom of Ukraine Has not yet Perished.

JAROSLAV

One of the first thing's you notice is how the average person behaves in public; if you try hard enough, you eventually get to understand why. Just as importantly, it doesn't take long to see how you need to act, should you ever want to fit in.

From a North American perspective, everything seems poised, slow, and old. The world, at least as I was explained back in Canada, is something that you craft to your own accord, based on what you do, how hard you work and, the x-factor no-one likes to admit, a large segment of luck. Still, if these ingredients are mixed right, with no sparing of what you can contribute, the odds of you being successful and making your mark in this world are far higher. At the very least, the idea within a North American mentality is that you have some control into how successful you will be, and where your hard work leads you is at least, within reason, partially in your control.

This is at odds with what I've been explained many times within the former Soviet bloc. The term that they use in defining their world is far more cynical; in fact, this mentality, as I mentioned once before, is often called "Soviet cynicism" and it can't be underestimated. One such example.

I knew a man called Jaroslav[7] that worked in a local hotel. In his mid twenties, highly intelligent, the man taught himself fluent English as to work in what little international business you find in Ukraine. Being from a poorer background, he worked in university to become an engineer, graduating with our equivalent of honours, and was set to work a field he was passionate for.

In Ukraine, no such ideas are realistic.

Yes, you will graduate with a degree of your choice. Yes, you will be able to demonstrate how hard you've worked, and yes, you will have theoretically earned your way into a better, brighter future. The problem with this mentality, to put it nicely, is that its utopic. For prospects to work this way in Ukraine, you would need something that far outstrips effort, intelligence, or even luck.

To begin with, there are no companies that will hire you.

By you, I mean Jaroslav, the son of a metal worker from some obscure oblast (province) that nobody knows about, nor cares to know. The same sort that files into the national polytechnic year in, year out, with all the credentials earned and acquired, that same person who has a similar sounding name to all others, the sort that wears a white shirt everyday to class, so that nobody knows that he owns all of two and his financial reality won't be obvious. Yes, to the mind of the few companies that could afford to hire an engineer, they are all the same, they do not matter.

Why they are like this is the same reason as why communism is evil. Communism poisons the mind, dulls the economic abilities of private corporations, and invites a bureaucratic monster that makes molasses seem fast. Most of all, the hypocrisy of such a system, one that supposedly levels the playing field for everyone, in reality adores money and the people that have any of it. Perhaps as perverse as the rest of it, even when a country leaves the land of gulags, this Soviet inspired mentality of bribery, corruption, and opaque governance permeates everything for generations to comes. So, while the Ukrainian SSR disappeared nearly thirty years ago, there is no doubt that the corrupt, bureaucratic ideals remain as strong as ever, with men and women my age or younger desperately trying to shed a mentality of old; one that thoroughly despises them and anything of the new.

Jaroslav is just such a victim. I picked him not because I think he's a decent person or because he stands out in any particular way; it's more because he's representative of what most Ukrainians have to go through, in order to make a half decent life.

Let's talk about clothes and phones.

In a country where the average salary is less than 400 CAD a month, you would think that luxuries such as an iPhone, designer clothing or jewelry would be exceedingly rare. Taking a walk in any Ukrainian city that has more than 100,000 people, you will notice that these items can be found everywhere and within the hands of most people over the age of fifteen. For men, you will have professional business attire, polished shoes and clean-shaven faces. They will walk with a measured, calculated stride of them, and in the more historical neighborhoods you could easily lose sight of where you are and believe, with reason, that you find yourself in the old quarters of Prague, Warsaw, or Budapest.

This is all illusory. None of what you see, from that initial glance, is representative of much.

Every morning I find Jaroslav in pressed clothes, wearing a skinny black tie, polished shoes, and a leather messenger bag that he places, neatly, on top of this knee length wool coat. His watch matches his leather belt, his wedding ring, on the left hand, denotes that he's Catholic, or rather, that he isn't Russian Orthodox. Through impeccably coiffed hair, disciplined mannerisms and English that is far better than certain parts of Montreal I used to live in, he is always proper, timed, and poised.

On his break, he will sit with a coffee and talk, one can eventually know the difference between Ukrainian and Russian just by hearing the syllables;

he eventual tells me that he is fortunate to have his current job. Unlike many, he doesn't smoke, and I've never seen him drink; as a result, his East European genes could make him pass as either someone is his early twenties or anything up to thirty-five, depending on how he dresses.

To continue on his tone and accent, it isn't just what he says that matters to me, or that makes him different from many other cultures I've seen in Eastern Europe; it's the way that he says it. When I ask a question, I can see that he's carefully considering his options, crafting an argument, and then gives a measured, paused statement[8]. It is rarely aggressive and tries to be diplomatic, aiming for agreeableness. I don't think it's even an attempt to be passive, I simply think that he's being careful when talking to people he neither knows well nor can trust.

His cell is an iPhone. It made me curious that in a country, at least so I read, where salaries are woefully low, how can it be that everyone dresses so well? Where is the poverty, I asked myself, looking at passersby in downtown Lviv, using dilapidated public transportation, yet dressed as if they're about to premier a theatre production, somewhere in Manhattan?

This is the first glimpse that was more than just the observation. For you to understand Ukraine, it can't be said clearly enough how much appearance and self-worth go hand in hand.

It starts in the morning, before the break of dawn.

Waking up before his wife and children, Jaroslav, like millions of Ukrainians, will quietly eat something before getting dressed in his carefully constructed wardrobe. This construction is designed so that he owns probably no more than two suits, three shirts, and wears them in such a manner, due to uniformity, that its plausible he has a much larger wardrobe than he actually does (that's the point). Never wearing the exact same thing twice in a row and re-organizing it so that it's plausible that his dress is simply professional, not sparse, he'll be leaving his house, probably owned by his parents,[9] no later than five thirty in the morning.

He will walk about fifteen minutes to half an hour to an obscure bus stop, board a highly packed, extremely quiet ride, and transit until he reaches a regional hub. From there, he will board a second, equally filled bus, where he will stop at another, this time urban transit point, leave, and walk some more. In general, he will commute anything from three to four hours a day, work for eight or nine, and do this process five or six days per week.

He will never complain, will never make noise, never discuss how far he lives or how tired he's become. Being a man, he will not have the luxury that women do in hiding their fatigue through carefully applied makeup. Yet, due to his neatly groomed appearance, to the casual observer it will simply look like he's just having an exceptionally long day. In fact, they are always, or just nearly, exceptionally long.

It isn't that he's hiding his situation, nor is it that he's trying to be something that he isn't. The clothes and the phone, items that he would have to budget for over a year, are not to gloat or to puff his allure. They are necessary for him to be presentable: North American slob acceptance does not pass. If you want to look like a tourist, all you have to do is dress like most people do in Canada, and you might as well have a sign in your forehead that says you're not Ukrainian.

When most people visit or work in Ukraine, their first impressions tend to be that their overall situation isn't that bad. Under some scrutiny though, you see how much it's the opposite. The way that you act and behave in public is synonymous with your value to society, and any liberties past this are very poorly seen.

Coffee for him is not done while walking, it isn't professional. You sit down and drink one, without the disposable cup. There's a saucer as well, and sugar cubes are a thing, not single serving packets.

You don't wolf down a sandwich while taking the bus, nor do you eat while walking. There's a time and place for this, known as a meal. You don't outstrip the convention.

When his wife came to the hotel for a Christmas party, I knew that he had borrowed a car from a colleague (it was modest). At arrival, he parks the car and opens the passenger door for his wife. It's normal, there are customs, they are worth it, they are not to be shunned. They exist for a reason.

He is quiet. He takes the time to carefully think about what he says before commenting. Life has taught him to measure carefully what he says in public, more so in front of people that he neither knows nor has a true idea of their status. A common theme between the Ukrainian mind and one that's Anglo-Saxon, a more accurate way to describe this would be a shared rule they have, is that all dirty laundry, so to speak, is done in private. In public, we don't talk negatively of others unless it's dire or very warranted.

Respect for tradition outstrips who you know or what you might gain from following convention. After this happened four times, I understood the following to be normal. In a large city, on a busy street, a funeral procession is taking place. Motorists that are passing by, that clearly wouldn't know the deceased, will immediately turn off their engines, get out of their cars, and take their hats off, as the hearse crosses their path. For a moment, life will stop for you as to pay respects to a stranger, not because you have something to gain; it is simply the right thing to do.

I made mention of this to Jaroslav, over one

of our conversations. I told him how respectful this behaviour is, that people maintain such values. Looking at me, in one of the few times I felt real resistance to my point of view, he asked me how someone could omit basic respect to the dead.

For most people in North America, in bygone times, we would do something similar. We would, so I'm told by my grandfather, have the unquestioned view to show a sign of respect to a grieving family, even if we don't know them. Looking at Jaroslav though, I had no answer that would paint my background as anything but selfish.

ANNA AND HER GRANDFATHER

A typical Ukrainian market. These are far more popular than commercial supermarkets in rural areas, due their lower cost and fresher goods.

My grandfather and I have a close relationship; there are few people (if any) that I respect more than him. When I returned from Ukraine, I remember sitting down with my grandparents and explaining what my impressions of Ukraine were, what their lives are like, and the paradox of their world next to mine. The paradox being that, while their lives are wildly different than those you typically find in Canada, there was this curious similarity between the way they live and something from my past that felt so, well, familial.

My grandfather would have been a good Ukrainian and I strongly suspect that this could be true for many of his generation. The parallel, after talking to common people became obvious, none more so than Anna.

Anna is a local teenager that worked at a store near a village I'd occasionally frequent. After school, she would help grandfather serve customers; the store was maybe the size of a small bedroom and sold items like instant coffee, cigarettes, and an energy drink called Nonstop.[10] Right beside this store, actually, more like in what seemed to be another room, a tastefully set up rest area of sorts was available for people to sit down and eat.

At 14 or so, she had taught herself English (it was impressively good) by watching YouTube and Sesame Street, happy to practice it with anyone.

Being Canadian, my stereotypical politeness came out and her quiet Ukrainian dignity was apparent in our multiple conversations. Either that, or I was one of the few English speakers that would frequent her store; I'd like to believe our time together was more than that.

Her grandfather knew that I was Canadian, and I think that this went a long way for me to converse with his granddaughter. At first, he was certainly curious as to why I would take interest in talking to her, past saying thank you. I saw that Anna explained to him that I'm part of the Canadian help to Ukraine, and it seems that his suspicions dissolved almost immediately. While I would have talked to her grandfather directly, he didn't speak English and my garbled Ukrainian wouldn't do, so Anna became both an interpreter and a teacher to me in how Ukrainian families live, how important they are to each other.

Anna was terrific in explaining the lives of average Ukrainians, so that's to say people who live in small villages, farming communities and in rural areas. Kyiv in Lviv, cities that I spent a lot of time in are simply not representative of the reality of most Ukrainians, and her insight was by far the best I had in understanding the more rural segment of their country.

On our first real conversation, her first question stumped me for at least half a minute. Alex, she said, why do Canadians grow grass?

Grass. You mean, as in a lawn? Why do we have lawns?

Yes. Why do you spend so much time growing a useless, inedible shrub, and waste so much space on a plant that does nothing? At least a flower garden looks nice and isn't boring. I mean, you cut it super short and has no features at all!

I couldn't offer her a decent answer.[11] It was one of those times where you get questioned on doing something that you've always taken for granted: you just never thought about why it matters. Why do we grow grass, I asked myself. Why did I spend a childhood mowing a useless plant, with a machine that my family bought solely for that purpose, offering us in turn nothing except maybe a version of what, proper esthetics? At the time, I couldn't really offer much, so I asked why lawns are not a thing in Ukraine.

Her reply was both logical and far more practical than my non answer, and it speaks to their overall mentality (or relationship) to things and money.

If you live in a village, the house you live in includes a small plot of land. So, why not use it to grow produce? It's no so much that money is rare (even though it is), its more on the basis that to do otherwise isn't logical. Why, wouldn't you take advantage of the space you have, and make your own food? Why depend on a store when you can simply learn to grow things? Basically, why wouldn't you maximize what you have?

This is opposite to what I know. As a hard guideline that has few exceptions, Canadians are consumers. We usually don't make our own things, grow our food, or build our houses. Generally, our relationships to material things are based on our salaries and our ability to spend to get what we want, or what we'd like. I'm sure that there was a time, at least two generations ago, when this wasn't the case for us; looking at Ukraine, their reality is that they have a much closer relationship to things they need, and it doesn't always pass through how much money they have.

There's a quality in what she wears and how she wears it. Her clothing, at least much of it, is clearly handmade, and it doesn't come off as a peasant girl look in the least; it looks high grade. Imagine embroidered motives overs a loose-fitting shirt, always with a geometric pattern of sorts- the first thought that comes to mind when you see these items is that someone spent real time crafting them. I'd imagine them lasting for years. She told me they come from her grandmother.

On the store that she manages with her grandfather. The interior is decorated with vegetables, smells of fresh spices, and it has an earthy feel in its décor that initially reminded me of Italy. It isn't lavish, nor ornate, it just comes off as handmade. The chairs, as I later found out, were carved by her brother, and the tables, all three of them, where made with trees that her grandfather cut down decades ago. Tables that used to be in storage now used to run a business. Everything in this little world seems to be either made by a family member or taken from nature within a ten-minute drive from where I stand. I swear, if I looked hard enough, I could probably find the sweat of her grandfather polished inside each one of these heavy, high-grade tables. More accurately, I'm sure that's what the grandfather would want me to find.

Money isn't dealt with in the same way. You know you're in Ukraine, or certain other parts of Eastern Europe, when cash isn't usually in the register, at least if you go to a family run business. On the part of women, I've noticed that they keep change/ earnings of the day in their purse: it seems the cash register is almost an accessory to ring up items though isn't used to keep actual money. So, if you give a larger bill,[12] they tend to rummage through their purse instead of the till- I never could figure out why that is. I asked Anna, and it seems that she was just as confused with we wouldn't do this in Canada, more convenient and safer she says. I think she's right.

Anna was telling me that village life is often a story of taking what exists in nature and making it your own; they're exceptionally talented at making things with their hands and they depend less on store bought items. Furniture, just like what I saw at her shop, is usually built from nearby trees, with the knowledge of skills taught from one generation to the next. The same can be said of quilts, shirts, you name it. There's pride in the creation of things that they use in daily life, something that felt foreign to me from my lived experience; it still made perfect sense in practice.

A typical Sunday for Anna's grandfather is to take a walk in the early hours of the morning, after tending to his animals. Not a large farm or anything; simply some chickens, maybe a goat; just something to complement their daily needs. In his morning walk, he'll likely step into the neighbouring forest, pick some mushrooms to complement a family meal, then maybe have coffee with his neighbor and friend of fifty years. Church would follow, then a nap, and then some time with his grandchildren. In all, a simple family life, build on the premise that what matters is each other, with little expectancy outside of their community.

Family bonds that you see in Ukraine, as their norm and especially outside of cities, are essentially obsolete in Canada. While I'm sure that there are exceptions, the bonds of trust that you see between family members in Ukraine, versus where I'm from, is something that most of us have lost.

I return now to my own grandfather, and his view is that this kind of life is exactly what we used to have in Canada. There wasn't as much of a dependency on government, the relationships most people had with politics were far. While there is a sentiment of pride in national identity (I speak here for Canada), it was certainly secondary to the identity people had with their village. The relationships we have now, versus those that were of another time, changed, according to my grandfather, drastically.

This brings me to Anna's grandfather, or my conversations with him.

As I was sitting in one of his handcrafted chairs, I had bought a storybook from a local shop and was trying my best to practice my reading skills. There were pictures that inferred that I was reading about traditional folk stories found in Ukraine, and it dawned on me rather quickly that Ukrainian, unlike English, is generally read exactly as spelled. Through my muffled muttering of syllables, passing by the fleeting "aha!" moment when I understood a full sentence, I saw Anna from the corner of my eye. Smiling, holding two cups of tea, she asked me if I would like to talk to her grandfather.

I had seen him at least at least a dozen times, and past saying hello (dobryy den), there really wasn't much interaction between the both of us. He would generally look at me talking to his granddaughter, nod once when I would walk in, and again when I would leave his shop, though it ended there. I immediately agreed, stood up to say hi, and he immediately gestured for me to sit down. Tea in hand, I knew that this was something that foreigners will rarely experience, and I know that this likely occurred only after a few months of him seeing me go about my business, knowing that I had time to spare for a conversation.

I should add, all of this happened through Anna, and for simplicities sake, I'm going to write this as if she wasn't there.

The first thing he asked me was why I was reading a storybook, more so in a language that I was barely able to grasp.

Well, as a guest of this country, it seems to me that the least I can do is try to understand something of Ukraine, its values, language, culture.

I've heard of Canadians doing such things, he replied. You like to learn things.

I do. And if you'd allow me, I'd like to know about you. I'd like to learn more about Ukraine.

His immediate reaction, as stoic as he may be, was one of confusion. Why I would care is the first concept we had to get through. I was toying for a moment that he was thinking I wanted to take advantage of him, was a police officer, or that I somehow would report him for an infraction of some kind. I had been in country for several months by then, so this sort of default of the part of a Ukrainian mind is more common than I would have ever thought. I explained to him, through simple examples, that I've worked in many different countries, and I always try to understand the people that live there, to honour the way that they see things, through talking and appreciating their values. This took time: I'm absolutely convinced that for the first five to ten minutes, he didn't believe a word I was saying. That I wasn't interested in money, gain, or some sort of self-gratification appeared very odd to him, totally foreign. In what almost (not quite) was coming off as lathering reassurance just a little too thick, he eventually gave me the words that I needed to hear.

Okay, he said, what would you like to know?

Tell me about Ukraine, and why you think that there is a struggle between mentalities of the old, and the promise of the new. Why do you think there's a difference between younger and older generations that is so pronounced here? His initial reaction to my question was a chuckle, and he started to tell me what he thinks.

Ukraine is a nation of farmers; it always had been. Looking at his mug, seemingly in deep thought, he explained to me that his family has been in Ukraine for at least eight or nine generations, and that he was told by his grandparents, generations ago, that they once originated from what we now call Poland. Much of what he told me I knew already.

Barring the hand painted eggs, borsh, and clothing, much of what we started with was routine. None of these talks mattered much, in contrast to what comes next. What was exceptional in my conversations with him is when we talked about how Ukrainians tend to view, to put it mildly, historical discrimination.

In the Western part of Ukraine, Jews were often in the majority, district wise at least, until the Second World War. Highly integrated, fluent in Ukrainian, Russian, and likely two other languages, Jews were an integral part of society. I use the past tense here, in that post 1945, there were essentially no Jews left.

The same could be said about Poles. Most of Western Ukraine, just by the look of it, can come off as more Polish than anything else: the names of the cities, the statues to the Pope that are littered everywhere- Roman Catholicism even, prevalent throughout both city and countryside. Yet, after less than three generations, there remains less than two percent of the population that speaks Polish, and it would be fair to say that what remains is either folkloric, historical, or very small, highly unrepresentative minorities.

The question isn't so much why it happened, for the purpose of our conversation, it was more how Ukrainians don't seem to care much about it. The purges are known- it simply seems that their history books and monuments to war (prevalent throughout society, let's be clear) are simply, to my mind, void of how minorities have been excluded or discriminated against. I was curious, in a non-judgemental way, to ask Anna's grandfather that question. And in the most carefully constructed way, one that I knew wouldn't cause offense, he was remarkably candid with me.

If I somehow haven't yet made this clear, history has not been kind to Ukraine. In Canada, the idea of a million of our citizens dying in less than a year is something we have never experienced. In Ukraine, this phenomenon occurred more than once or twice, and it was simply part of another bloody chapter of being caught between juggernauts. Be it on the part of the USSR, the Third Reich, or the USSR for another half century, there are no limits to the amount of suffering that you can find via a Google search on Ukraine.

This was exactly how he started to explain why there is so little empathy in his country. For the Holodomor, a genocide that has virtually no attention on the worldwide stage, the level of empathy Ukraine gets from international community is essentially zero. The Russian Federation still denies it as a genocide, Ukrainian oligarchs in power a recent Ukrainian president downplayed the events ad nauseum, there is little empathy for their struggles. It is remembered as a deeply painful event, and the lived memory of those much older recall their parents and grandparents describing it in shushing tones in the privacy of their homes. Remember: it was a crime to even talk about it, for decades on end.

If there is so little attention given to their own struggles, how, said the grandfather, can we be expected to have any for others? How can anyone expect me, or people like me, he said, sipping on his tea, to care more about a minority, whatever minority it is, when we have a hard time even recalling, never mind caring, about the level of pain we ourselves have lived through?

And if you think that this is somehow justifying discrimination, think again. In the same breath, or almost so, he was categoric that there was no justification for the discrimination, ethnic cleansing, or all out genocide that Ukrainians participated in. These actions are, to be crystal, overwhelmingly viewed as appalling and they are not denied. They are simply, how about that, another horror in a show of horrors. To be blunt, he said something along the lines of six million dead is unthinkable, now imagine a people going through a number twice as high.

On our second conversation, we pivoted to talking about cities, or rather, the lack of appeal they have for many rural residents. For many regions, that there isn't the of exodus one could expect towards them. Population wise, many have remained constant, and their way of life is often unchanged. To give you an example: you can find dirt roads throughout Ukraine that appear to be narrow, almost too narrow for a car. Here's why: those roads are still used by horses, mainly because they're fair cheaper than using gas.

Also, it's not that they don't know about the

city life; many try, and it often happens that they don't like it. Anna's brother was an engineer by education, and, realizing that the salary for his profession was very low (to include giving an honest try of about two years), he figured that there is no real future in a corporate world. So, he returned to his village and started to work on engineering projects, all of them low key, as to develop and practice sustainable farming. Anna's brother now does irrigation projects related to collective farming, the small profits going to his family and neighbors.

While it might be slowly fading (this is a guess, I don't know for sure), rural Ukrainians have a profound sense of belonging to their oblast, village, and family home. While there is an openness to difference, certainly from my observations there are few reasons for them to leave what is a quiet, and all things considered, quite wonderful, family life behind.

PIOTR

Piotr was a 24-year-old from the south-west tip of Ukraine. Shorter than most military officers, he left university after his degree and joined the army almost immediately after Maidan. From a family of merchants, Piotr had the opportunities that few would ever have: a solid business to inherit, a family that was doing financially well and, just as importantly, a name with a reputation that would allow him to continue developing what his grandfather started.

Like most, he was a man of very, very few words. Introverted to the point of questioning if he wanted to talk to you, his words were measured, carefully chosen, and always done with the cautious understanding that you can make adversaries far easier than friends. While he knew that Canadians are in Ukraine to help, he also knew its possible we'll go away while his country is still fighting a war. Coffee in hand, with a cigarette smoked to the cut, he would carefully pause every time someone asked him a question, qualifying his remarks to a T.

And like all Ukrainian men that I met, pride,

or rather, not looking weak was a highly prized, important aspect to him. The issue: his soldiers lacked winter clothing and due to a backlog issue (or so I was told) Piotr was concerned that his men might freeze. Logistics, he says, can take a long time in his country[13] and his staff might have to do without.

To then we insert what I'll qualify as a foolish idea. One of the Canadians stationed at the same base as Piotr thought of a great idea; in it of itself, it was exactly so. Knowing that Canadians always travel with too much equipment, it was easy to muster, so he told me, a few hundred additional sets of winter gear for Piotr's crew. A phone call and one signature later, the Canadian had all that his Ukrainian counterpart would ever need, and proudly walked to Piotr's office, as to tell him the good news.

Walking into a government office, the Canadian opens the main door and finds the neatly organized desk that Piotr uses to staff his assignments and training duties. There, in front of a dozen other Ukrainian officers, the Canadian makes a modestly public announcement of what he thinks is a good deed. The response was as quick as the offer, by which I mean it took less time for the reply to come than the presentation of that seemingly good deed.

No thank you, said Piotr.

We have no need for what you offer.

Again, I thank you for your thought.

Returning to the Canadian side of things, he

looks at me and tells me this story. How could a man, no later than yesterday, be so frigid in my offer of goodwill? What could motivate someone in need to refuse equipment so sharply, knowing full well that his men will freeze over the coming winter months?

The answer lies in culture.

In Ukraine, weakness is never rewarded. While vulnerability and piety may be morally acceptable virtues in North America, in a country where there are no second chances and where your name is all that matters, and I do mean ever, to offer something, anything in such a way is unthinkable. It would translate to something like this:

Hey Piotr, I know that your government is so miserably pathetic that it can't clothe your guys for the wintertime. So how about this: I asked around and it took me a phone call and ten seconds of my superior's time to get more than you could in a month. So how about it? Oh also, I'll announce this in front of everyone as to make you look extra weak and insubordinate; I'm sure nobody will think that you went to me begging or anything. So, we good Piotr? Can I get a medal?

I was extra careful in explaining the following to the Canadian: I know you meant well, yet your presentation is a solid F. For you to work with Ukrainians, you must understand the background and realities that they come from. In turn, they will work with you.

What then, asks the Canadian.

Have a colleague, not you, go back to Piotr in a week. Have the colleague ask him for advice. In this advice, have the colleague mention how you have a large amount of equipment, and you don't know what the best way would be to share resources, from one ally to the next. Who do I see? What do I do? What would the process be? Make it a large blanket statement of advice asking, in such a way that it would be impossible for you to know how to do your assigned task right, without Piotr's help.

Piotr will offer his insight and will expand on various concepts of administration that are so bland that boredom happens within a minute. Ask some more questions, take some notes, and thank him for his time. For that day, leave the conversation after a coffee and a cigarette- might I add that it would be a good idea to ask Piotr for all of this in the same spot that the Canadian did: in front of his peers, in front of his superiors. Do not be deferent, do not theatricalize the scene, do not be ridiculous. If you do, I promise you Piotr will never want to hear about clothing again.

The next day, return to Piotr, this time asking him for a favour. He'll gladly say yes, and then explain to him that, based on your conversation, it seems like no small task to allocate stores. Would he, the good Ukrainian, do you the favour of distributing this equipment, through whatever channels he deems to be the most appropriate?

This is important: make no mistake that Piotr knows exactly what you're doing. He isn't stupid, and he understands perfectly well that you're giving him the position of authority he needs. By acting this way, you've been able to appreciate his situation; in return, several dozens of men will be warm over the winter.

Dignity and pride can't be overstated. If you think Piotr is unrepresentative, there was once a class of Ukrainian soldiers that were being taught by a Canadian on how to navigate with NATO grade maps. One of the training aids went missing, and so the Canadian asked the Ukrainian supervisor if anyone might have taken it. That ask, in public no less, would have resulted in all the Ukrainian students being strip searched for said aid, and God help whoever had it hidden in their pocket. I suspect a beating would be in order, likely more. Thankfully, it was an honest mistake: the training aid fell to the ground between two floorboards, and it was clear that nobody was trying to steal.

A military clergyman frequents a village not too far away where the average income is less than 250 CAD a month. At the end of the visit, the mayor invites him to have a meal to celebrate Canadian and Ukrainian ties. The bill was not cheap.

Do you think it's even possible for that clergyman to pay his share?

Maybe I should re-frame how hard life is in

Ukraine. Taking an example that has nothing to do with a Canadian interaction, consider what they will do to each other when foreigners aren't around. An American once told me, when I was in Kyiv, that one of the best paramilitary forces in Ukraine, considered better than the regular military, caught one of its soldiers stealing money from the unit. It was in the order of about five hundred American dollars, a sum nearly unthinkable to the average Ukrainian. To be clear: they were certain that the soldier stole the money. To be even clearer, what I'm about to tell you is extreme and, this level of severity, even in Ukraine, is generally frowned upon. War generally tends to lighten ethics.

A pit was dug with a depth of at least ten meters, maybe four meters wide. The soldier was thrown in and left for weeks on end; he was never removed. For food, staff from his unit, having a measure of pity, would occasionally toss scraps at him with whatever else they thought they could spare. No change of clothes, rain would accumulate to the tune of several inches, natural waste remained there, to dry in the sun, to moisten in the morning.

I can only imagine the smell, the anger, the fear, the total depravity that must have been at the bottom of that pit. I'm certain that the smell must have been so bad that, after a few weeks, those that so much as walked near that pit were about to pass out. Yet, this was just the beginning.

When he was finally removed from his impromptu cell, after what I'm assuming was a shower of some kind, he was stripped of his uniform, rank, and prohibited from ever serving again. He was forced to walk home, from a warzone, over a distance that would require several days, maybe even more than a week. Upon arriving at his village, the staff from his former unit made sure that his high school teachers, clergy, and parents were fully aware of why he was banned from serving his country and detailed in great length the reason.

There is no easy way for this soldier to ever make amends with what he has done. He stole from his unit, his community, his country. His theft, if unfound, would have resulted in less munitions, clothing, and food as to keep fighting. He is unacceptable, unworthy, and will have the shame of his consequences hanging over his head for the foreseeable future. Unforgiveable, unacceptable, shameful. He will pay a high price; in a country at war, the cost, in Ukraine and at the time, was just about fitting.

Stubborn to excess, proud to no end, the Ukrainian mind operates on a few simple principles, and it would be too easy to say that power is a motivator. It is, from my perspective, a mix of my grandfathers very Catholic pride, combined with the quiet, measured reactions best found in Eastern Europe. In this, one of their paramount's is easily found: Piotr in this sense is but a result of his country, his culture.

So goes a Ukrainian proverb, no matter how

hard you try, the bull will never give milk. Should you fail to understand how important pride is for them, I promise you this: not only will you get no milk, that bull might decide that's it's fed up of you trying...

SASHA

At the height of his (maybe) five feet four, 130-pound frame, my first impression was that he's had a hard life. His teeth and what was left of his right ear had seen better times, to put it mildly, and while the medical staff where I was living would never tell me directly, it seemed clear that he was one of many that, due a rough childhood, had the obvious scars of malnutrition. I'm told such scars are permanent.

Sasha was one of thousands that was deployed to the eastern part of Ukraine to fight against Russian Led Separatist Forces (RLSF). Some context as to why the world almost universally refers to the ongoing fighting within Ukraine as being a proxy war with Russia should be our starting point.

As outrageous as it may seem, the Russian Federation maintains, as I write this, of having nothing to do with the ongoing fighting in the eastern part of Ukrainian territory, at least from the standpoint of armed involvement. Their party line is that is that ethnic Russians are oppressed by the Ukrainian oligarchs in Kyiv, and that when Donetsk and Luhansk attempted to separate from Ukraine, the Russian Federation offered only economic and limited political support. For extra clarity, the Russian Federation has flatly denied ever sending soldiers, weapons, or equipment to fight the Ukrainian military.

Quite a coincidence when you think of it. Just as Maidan was happening in Kyiv, where the puppet, pro-Russian government du jour was summarily ousted from office and self-exiled to Russia, just then was when the beginning of warfighting within the ATO.

Material evidence, no matter how one looks at it, couldn't be more at odds with the Kremlins official standpoint. To illustrate the absurdity of their claim, Russian soldiers have been repetitively caught by the Ukrainian army deep within the ATO wearing sanitized uniforms (so no nametags, unit patches and the like), as to obfuscate their identities. Due to the glaring contradiction of what they say versus what's happening, the Kremlin even went so far as to say that yes, maybe some of their soldiers are fighting in Donetsk or Luhansk, although these were personal choices. So goes the argument, some Russian soldiers prefer to spend their vacation time assisting fighters in the ATO instead of going to the black sea with their families.[14]

Even more absurd is what I saw in front of the Great Patriotic War Museum in Kyiv, dedicated to Second World War. As a sign of proof, the Ukrainian military displays a tank captured in Ukraine that was never part of their stockpiles. The tank's description goes so far as to detail to the unit it belongs to in Russia, the equipment stored within it, and simple, cursory internet searches show that Ukraine has never owned such a vehicle. This is not a story of a few trainers, small arms, or some logistical support (all of which isn't supposed to exist): this is material evidence of multimillion-dollar war machines operating in the ATO, curtesy of the Russian military. If nothing else, the cost alone of these tanks would make it impossible for an insurgency force, from one of the poorest areas of Ukraine, to purchase them. In one sentence: there are no options that come close to reality except that these war machines came from Russia.

One would have to be brainwashed to believe that the Russian Federation isn't actively undermining the attempts of Ukraine to maintain its sovereignty, and this includes armed assistance to the RLSF within the ATO. While that's the most common sense argument, another, slightly less obvious one, is the clear intent to prohibit Ukraine from even joining the European Union.

Sasha had been fighting in the ATO for at least ten months. The Ukrainian military, one that has doesn't have the luxury of Russian equipment or technologies, combined with a very minimal number of stockpiles, has been bravely defending its sovereignty with almost nothing. To equate the Russian and Ukrainian military would probably be like comparing the might of United States to Canada; there is no real comparison.

A T-64BV Main Battle Tank. At that time, Ukraine never had such a vehicle within its arsenal, and through equipment tracing no doubt exists: it belongs to the 205th Motorized Brigade of the Russian Federation. Captured in the ATO and now displayed in Kyiv, it exists to counter propaganda with proof.

In a Western military, the general guideline is that an overseas deployment is for a period of 6 to 12 months, with one, preferably two, short vacations. Afterwards, you would then be sent home, exhausted, and left alone to recover for a month or two. After that, the average serviceperson would be given garrison related activities, so something administrative, with the understanding that they'd return home everyday. There is a particularly good reason for this kind of treatment, and it has nothing to do with kindness.

Previous conflicts have shown that the more you work your staff, the more they break down, and the less people, certainly those of high quality, remain as to continue a given deployment. Of this I'm certain: several armed forces throughout the world would view this as a weakness, and it would be the same ones that still struggle with the notion of having a professional army. I won't name them.

Because they're at war and need everyone they have, Ukrainian soldiers lack vacation time. The facts are clear: they're at war with a larger, far more powerful armed force and they simply don't have the means to offer their soldiers a break. It's not that they're soulless, nor is it that they don't care about their people; they simply don't have the ability to give them the rest and the resulting increase in morale.

Returning to Sasha, his overall appearance when he arrived in Western Ukraine was telling. From my experience, extremely dishevelled, exhausted men come into these training centers with uniforms that, if I didn't know better (...), seem to have been issued a day before their arrival. They have circles under their eyes that reach to their cheekbones, say nothing, eat, and disappear for a few days in barracks that many Canadians share with them, barring different floors. Sasha was one of these men, in a sea of quiet soldiers that would shuffle from their barracks, nod politely to us, and, over time and linguistic clumsiness on our part, slowly open to those curious.

I will never know if being trained by Canadians was a privilege to be earned, although I strongly suspect this was the case. Considering their pay that can barely cover the cost of cigarettes, that they are initially issued one uniform[15] and their training is but a matter of weeks before going to a warzone, to be out of the ATO is surely a luxury.

And tired is the best way for me to convey what they looked like. For a few days, I don't think I saw many of them even leave their sleeping quarters, and despite not knowing for sure why, I can safely say that this is related to what must be very hard military service.

This is when trainers learn how to work with Sasha, but more importantly, how not to.

Like most East Europeans, Sasha is incredibly careful with what he says. If there is a doubt to what he should say, or if there is a chance that it will contradict someone in a position of authority, he generally won't say a thing. Do not confuse this with weakness or a lack of moral courage: nothing could be further from the truth. This is a culture where you do what you are told and authority is rarely, if ever, questioned. To his mind, that he is quiet and non-confrontational goes with his understanding of respect.

This might not appear to be a problem, although I guarantee you that it was the source of real frustration for trainers. For instance, let's say that the lesson du jour is to show soldiers how to attack and capture a building.[16] The trainer explains, demonstrates, and in turn, with the aid of an interpreter, makes sure that everyone understands. Questions anyone? Sasha? No? Okay, let's go practice how to attack and capture that building.

It does not go well.

It's like they weren't even listening, thinks the trainer, and the reaction I've heard time and time again goes like this:

They're a mess, everyone is waiting to be told something, dammit, just kick the door in! Why are you all staring at each other, waiting to be told what to do! Why didn't you ask me if you didn't understand, instead of just staring at me?

In the West, be in policing, paramedics, and especially soldiering, we naturally give people, regardless of their rank, at least some independence in what they do. If a leader told their subordinate to drive fifteen minutes ahead and see what the terrain looks like, it would be normal, and expected, that if there was something just a minute or two past what they were told to look at, they could do so. Basic initiative would be how most Westerners would see this kind of action, and it I'd argue that if someone didn't at least get the point of what they're being asked (i.e., the purpose of you being told to scout something is to see if there's anything!), there would be a conversation to be had.

For Ukraine, and this is a legacy of the USSR, that is not how they're trained. Fifteen minutes? That person will drive exactly fifteen minutes, and any deviation of what was ordered tethers on insubordination, and certainly is not valued within their understanding of following instructions. They are conditioned to follow exactly what they are being told, finish the job fully and completely, and then report back, period.

When being trained, the reason why they're confused and aren't doing what you explained is because they don't understand what you're talking about. What you showed them is radically different from what they're used to, and to tell you otherwise would be rude. To ask you to explain it again would be rude. In fact, to do anything except be quiet while you talk would be rude. Questions from them to the trainer, without previous approval? Rude.

To a Canadian mind, the liberties in the way we speak to authority are natural. Such notions, at least culturally, are anathema to a Ukrainian. They do not allow confusion to overstep a very clear understanding of respect. This might sound odd, yet I can assure you that this is not going to change anytime soon. Also, you can't try the "talk to me like I'm your friend" or "really people, you can just ask me if you don't get it." That will not do.

Here's how you can work well with Sasha. Let's say you want to show him how to drive a manual car (even though most vehicles in Ukraine are manual, though that's beyond the point). Show him the stick, tell him about pressing the pedal and shifting, and then give him the keys.

While he's not going to do a good job the first time, he'll learn through making mistakes and applying what works. From instructors telling me how they dealt with the cultural divide, it would be fair to say that Ukrainians, generally, are not interested in abstract concepts, theory or vagaries that are not logical. So, to say that they're hands on learners is a minimum: if you think PowerPoint is ineffective to North Americans, Ukrainians will stare blankly as you talk, absorbing little.

A translator told me one their favourite jokes.[17] This one is through Sasha.

A Ukrainian wakes up on a small, deserted island, when a magic fish swims up to the shore. He's a golden magic fish you see, and he grants three wishes to anyone he choses. In this case, the lucky shipwrecked Ukrainian is chosen by this magical, golden fish.[18]

I would like the Chinese army to invade Ukraine, and once they have, return immediately to China.

Confused, the golden magic fish shrugs and grants the wish. The entirely of the Chinese military crosses the continent, invades Ukraine, and once occupied, immediately returns to China.

That was your first wish, says the magic fish. What would be your second?

I want the Chinese army to do the same thing, all over again.

Well, all right, responds the magic fish. Looking at the Ukrainian in a rather confused way for a minute of two, he nonetheless grants the odd wish, one that's the same as the first. Sure enough, the Chinese army crosses the continent once more, invades Ukraine, and leaves almost immediately after, heading back to China.

Done, says the golden magic fish. What would be your third wish?

I want the Chinese military to-

Wait. Hold on, says the magic fish. Usually, people ask me for money, or youth, or a device with magical powers. Don't get me wrong, I'll grant your wish. I must ask though, why is it that you want the Chinese army to invade Ukraine and then leave right away, at that three times in a row?

Without pause, the Ukrainian smiles and says only one thing.

When this happens, that means the Chinese army had to invade Russia six times...

THERE IS NO YUGOSLAVIA

In the early nineties, one of the very few instances of something that looked like functional communism fell apart. A state neither aligned with NATO, nor really with the Warsaw Pact, Yugoslavia was one of the few (if not the only) communist states where citizens were free to leave as they pleased, travel was not curated and their dictatorship, in comparison to most, was not as soaked in blood. Yes, the dictatorship of Tito Broz, while it had its secret police and roundups, followed by secret trials and detentions, remained a state where at least three groups of people that historically despised one another got along for decades. A Croat, Tito was at least respected by Serbs and not always due to his power; for anyone with knowledge of this part of the world, that is an extraordinary feat.

Often viewed as a pearl of culture, literature, and, to my knowledge, the only state that was able to stave off any of Stalin's annexations,[19] it stood alone in the world. In fact, after one assassination attempt, Tito told Stalin that if he ever tried that again, he'd have him killed by sending his own assassins to Moscow. I could go on: suffice it to say that Yugoslavia was really something, more so for its time.

One of thousands of posters in markets throughout Ukraine. They won't sell products from the Russian Federation. This has nothing to do with Russian culture, or its people

Yet, in the early nineties when the Yugoslav republic dissolved, it did not take long for ancestral animosities to return. From an era of relative peace and tranquility, what has often been described as the largest ethnic cleansing since the Second World War, within Europe, occurred over a period of less than five years. This was not in the third world, nor in a warring state that was fractured decades ago; this all happened in a country that bordered Italy. The estimates of casualties, by all sides during the dissolution of the Yugoslav republic, can be counted in the millions. One of the results was Serbia became a willing tributary to Russia, Croatia to the European Union, and a language that had never used Cyrillic in the past suddenly began to do so. All of this was based almost exclusively on tribalism, which is to say through language, religions, and identity. Yet for forty years, practically none of this mattered to Yugoslavs, at least not to the point of murdering their fellow countrymen. Sadly, the time to hate one another swiftly returned: barbaric practices Europe swore to itself would never be seen again surfaced in a matter of weeks.

While this might not seem related to Ukraine, nothing could be further from the truth. Yugoslavia is a country remembered in Ukraine as a cautionary tale. To them, Yugoslavia is the demonstration of what can happen when two or more cultures no longer agree to prosper together. The result: a return to primitive, primal views that conclude in slaughter.

When I was in Ukraine, one of the first naïve (maybe the word I'm looking for is uneducated) questions that I asked was regarding the Russo-Ukrainian connection- how they get along so well. From my initially, and woefully simplistic grasp of Ukrainian history, correlated with fighting in the ATO, the assumption that I was buying into is that Russians are to blame.

For an outsider, this is one of the most monstrous mistakes you can make. Let me pause on this: the very worst thing you can do is correlate the simplistic idea that former soviet bloc states hate Russians as a people, and that Ukrainians surely despise them as well.

If you were to take Ukraine and cut it in half, geographically speaking, most of the country, east of the Dnieper, speaks Russian at home, is Orthodox by religion and by most ways you could measure it are culturally Russians. At the same time, they are Ukrainian by both citizenship and allegiance and as result, that the Russian Federation happens to be full of Russians becomes irrelevant. If I take myself as an example, the fact that I speak English and have somewhat comparable values to an Australian or an American does not change my identity or loyalty to Canada. For reasons that aren't entirely clear to me, the West has a tendency of being simplistic with such things when it comes to the Russian diaspora.

In turn, what you have is a unified, multilingual mass of citizens that rally under the Ukrainian flag. They abhor the Russian Federations interventions to the point of willing to die to save their state, although this should never be confused with Ukrainians having a problem with Russians as a people. Ukrainians that are culturally Russian are equal in value to the majority, and the idea that they are somehow now a foreign presence is something that I never heard of, nor witnessed. There may be some fools, somewhere in Ukraine that correlate Russian culture with the government of the Russian Federation, although I can't stress enough how I never saw such a thing.

At least a dozen times, locals would tell me about Yugoslavia as the perfect example of what not to do. That Ukraine is fighting for its very survival in the face of a juggernaut, and yet maintaining this clear policy of inclusivity, from my perspective, is very impressive. There are no shortages of instances when warfighting, corruption, and religious differences threaten the existence of a nation; I could cite examples that span anything from Chechnya to Northern Ireland.

And to its credit, Ukraine is not a nation that became divided on linguistic and/or ethnic lines.

So, when politicians in Ukraine voted to remove Russian as a national language, my view is that this was a mistake. To what are probably the hundreds of people that I talked to during my stay in their country, I never found one person that agreed with that idea. I understand that this is a political statement: the Russian Federation has no place within Ukraine, and by removing what is a common language between both countries, a point on sovereignty is made. I get that. Yet, this is not doing a service to the millions of brave Ukrainians that are culturally Russian and unapologetically patriotic about their citizenship, identity, and land.

In all of this, we must remember that it is never Russian culture, identity, or language that's the problem. While Ukrainian and Russian culture are distinct from one another, to use the term that's so often said in both countries, they are brothers. Both are profoundly family based, extremely hard working, and loyal to their families to no end. These are people that are brilliant in their studies, have abilities in mathematics that North America lags far, far behind, and the Russian Federation, as a state, is not Russian culture.

My own view, as I'm sure has been made clear by now, is that the current government of the Russian Federation is doing no service to its people, and its very unfortunate that we, in the West, often confuse both concepts and assume they are the same. A Russian will work without complaint, will struggle to provide without excuse, and will have values so clearly enshrined as to never question them. These are honourable characteristics found in both Ukrainian and Russian culture that are independent from political systems. Both cultures are honourable and serve as an example to me as what a nation can do through ridiculous adversity. Both deserve, on equal footing, our respect.

There is no Yugoslavia.

BEARS

Mild caution: I wrote this travelling in one of the poorest areas of Western Ukraine. This is not representative.

I walked into a small shop in the southwest part of Ukraine yesterday, in a village that was particularly poor. Just like many, during the daytime they keep the lights off to save money, so even if you have the opportunity to be in a store that's got windows, its hard to fully see what they have. The smell is the first thing that I notice; it isn't a rank, putrid odour or anything, more of a very light hint of vegetables that have been in the sun too long, often with a mix of dried, salted fish. Just enough to make you think twice about buying anything quote unquote fresh: you suddenly find yourself doubting what might be safe to eat, and a mild fear of getting poisoned and/or sick starts to sink in.

The small things, always the small things. You know that a place is poor when they keep toilet paper and milk behind the counter, contained in glass display cases that look to be fifty years old; it prevents someone from pocketing an egg without paying. The entire cost of something that is so precious, I am not being sarcastic here, the shopkeeper lives off selling these items, maybe fifteen Canadian cents for a roll of toilet paper, ten cents for an egg. Everything under lock and key, so to speak, with a woman probably in her thirties that looks to be sixty making sure that nobody takes from her store, which is directly and immediately the same as stealing from her family and her ability to live, pardon, to survive the reality of being a poor Ukrainian.

Somehow, no matter how I dress and how I try to imitate the way that they walk and look at people, it only lasts about thirty seconds before they know that I am not from their world. Maybe it's the fact that I still use my Western body language no matter how hard I try; they are stoic, I am not. A nod at someone on the street and they know you aren't from there, a smile to somebody (that one I haven't done in a long time) and there you go, you are no longer part of them. Is it the way that I walk with a sense of purpose, that I occasionally look elsewhere but straight ahead, maybe have a non-neutral facial expression that gives me away? I have no idea although I know that shopkeeper sure did.

After what was probably less than a minute, she stopped scanning me and looked at everyone else. Yes, you now know that I won't steal from you.

The small blond boy beside me looking up with his mouth slightly open, with his neutral expression, his mom holding his hand as she's looking at a large sack of spices, I'm assuming for her family's daily soup. Everything here is like a slow, sad dream: it feels like I am stuck in 1983 in the USSR somewhere, as the village shopkeeper prevents "accidents" from happening (i.e., people stealing). In but a few words, it feels poor and tethers on desperate. I think that Ukrainians are simply too proud to admit their state.

I buy a chocolate bar for 9 Hryvnas which would translate to something like fifty cents and pocket it immediately. I saw the blond boy looking at what I bought, me placing the bar in my pocket, to then seeing his mom tug his hand so that he would stop looking at me. Don't you dare look at him or his luxury, what will others think if you appear poor or in want. I suspect hunger was part of this, maybe. I thank the shopkeeper and she mutters you're welcome, in truth my Canadian manners are neither relevant nor are they appropriate. At that time, I wasn't certain: is it that I love to hate, or maybe that I hate to love, the sad wonder of this country. Without knowing exactly how they feel about me, I know that being totally alien is part of their impressions.

My colleague and I go for a walk in this town. Dilapidated buildings from the early eighties are just peeling away, the graffiti or the rotting sidewalks that are essentially granules of concrete lifted by my shoes, the grass just encroaching in their dissolving public structures is everywhere. Their national flag is very present: yellow and blue and most are tattered and worn from being in the sky for so long, a symbol I suppose of days that they wished would eventually come.

The epiphany of my day was this:

At first it was nothing really, it was a wood carving of two cubs playing with a porcupine; the one closest was, in a very subtle sense, smiling. The building in the background was typical for that town, so falling apart with graffiti, to include bricks that were either removed or fell naturally, then removed. The bears however, I thought someone must have spent a lot of time to carve these out of wood; there is real talent in whoever did this with a simple slice of life example that you might almost find in nature.

That bear's smile was the only one I saw that day. The bears playing, that was something that someone, somewhere with real talent did for others. I bet that person received no money for the effort, placing his art in front of yet another decrepit government compound to try to bring some joy to passers by, to locals that would see something that might make them smile.

I show this because, to me, going on my fourth month of being in Ukraine, that this is the most accurate photo I have yet taken that summarizes the state that these people are in. Here is a country with almost nothing going, no money, no opportunity, that you would be tempted to dismiss almost immediately after having taken one honest look, and then, almost at the last second, there is that slight glimmer of hope that you find somewhere. I can't tell you exactly what that hope is, nor can I stress enough how small it must be, though there is something that is keeping these people from abandoning any idea of a future. Somewhere in that carving of those two bears and a curious porcupine, I found a clue to where that hope might be.

THE POOR

I've noticed that the quality of public transportation (barring subways), tends to be a good indicator of how much money a state has.

Poverty is an extremely relative term, and throughout my adult life, I've lived, worked, or transited through at least half a dozen states that would qualify, without question, as being in dire straits. For Ukraine, poverty is something that is hard to find on the surface: if you were to travel for a few days throughout large cities, you would likely not see much of it, and this is chiefly because they will hide (and well) indicators of decay. I don't blame them; were I in a similar position, I would do the same.

Yet, the reality of their society, after living in country for a few weeks, becomes glaring. Were I to try to describe this via a metaphor, it would be like walking into a butcher shop and noticing a mild stench. Then, as you close the door, the odour becomes progressively so obvious you can barely pretend that you aren't sharing in the reek. I am not calling these people animals, what I am saying that they often have no choice but to, from a Canadian perspective, be treated as one, to act like one. It sickens me that they must act this way; that there's nothing that I can do about it makes it worse.

The treatment of the elderly poor is particularity difficult to understand; not just from others, but how they treat themselves. I'm told families generally don't know about what I'm about to tell you; I remain extremely pessimistic and suspect this more a case of not wanting to know, more than anything else. I'll never be sure. What I do know is that seniors are expected to somehow survive on a pension that would total less than 60 Canadian dollars a month and nowhere, I mean nothing in the realm of possibility, makes it plausible to eek out an existence with such limited funds. So, what do these elderly people do? They sell, they beg, they are condemned to something far lower than a standard of decency. It is, simply, their humanity that's for sale; it is extremely cheap.

In but a word troubling. It would be more accurate to say that I am deeply disturbed in seeing these things. Maybe it's because of my parents and how they raised me to treat my elders, maybe it's just a first world problem in appreciating just how desperate the rest of the planet is. Maybe I am soft, maybe I am weak. Maybe.

I go into a local market and see what the average person will sell, by which I mean the elderly poor. They will travel several hours to get to a location, then a few hours back to make roughly one hundred or so Hryvna, so less than ten dollars. When they arrive, they will empty their pockets of their goods, which is something like three cabbages, a bottle of goat's milk and a handful of radishes. That ten dollars does sound extremely inflated, now that I contextualize. They will place them on a napkin or a small white towel and they stand behind it quietly, watching people come near them. They will rarely talk or make any noise; they just stare at you. I have yet to see any of them sell whatever below meagre goods they have. I would say I have no idea why they try, except that I know that they do because they have no other choice. This is their life.

This is not a pity case, yet. Those with their small, pathetic number of wares will be somehow, I think, be empowered (that isn't the right word) in that they will have this thing, this something that belongs to them. In this, they might be able to say to their families when they return home that they were busy...working? In truth, I have no idea what they would say, except that whatever it is, it wouldn't be the truth. Those are the lucky ones. The rank fish and peeling meats with flies on them, the dark alleys with row after row after row of these old, nutcracker still people, those are the ones that are the most fortunate.

They are the ones who look at you with glazed, glossed over eyes, the ones that say almost nothing but a whisper, probably due to senility. If I took a picture then or in 1979 it would probably show the exact same pose from identical people, mutter potentially excluded. That is the fortunate elderly when we talk about the poor.

Those who are not beg. They sit on cold floors of peeling concrete and rain, in very used, extremely tattered clothing, it is always women who are at this level of abject and they mutter so that you can maybe hear something if you try hard. They adorn a religious postcard that they take out of their pocket with some Cyrillic written under it, I don't need to read their language to understand the gist. There they are muttering, speaking softly, staring at the floor with a small napkin with change that wouldn't total a quarter combined. It was sad to the point that my "learned" Ukrainian stoicism was rapidly fading. It almost went away when I saw that one of them looked almost exactly like my grandmother; this bothered me beyond a descriptive.

Most who cross their path act as if they don't see them and, to be fair, maybe you can reach a point where you don't. Except for whispers, these grandmothers say truly little as they clutch their used postcards with soft, frail hands that visibly tremble from a distance. There is so little chance that this is staged, the likelihood is that this is real. They incarnate their God through a barely audible request to be alleviated of their miseries, if but for the day, as they look blankly at the cold wet pavements in front of them. More than once in the space of ten paces, my heart sank, and sank. And sank.

The men do not beg, they sell. An old man who must have been 85 was in front of me with very thin arms and a leather jacket, where the sleeves were at least six inches too short. He had a length of twine around his neck which held a small pail that was filled with walnuts. Assumingly, he was selling them by the unit, shuffling from one spot to the next, muttering, dazed, oblivious. In this perverse display, I couldn't help but realize just how different I would seem to them if they knew who I was; I sort of look like their grandchildren, perhaps, and so long as I demonstrate no signs of reaction to what I see, it would appear that I, pardon me, fit in with this.

When I returned to an isolated place my better half told me that my alumni had sent me a letter for a reunion. Considering what I'm seeing here, I'm not sure which one feels real.

A SNAPSHOT OF WOMEN

The average Ukrainian shopping mall. Imagine a labyrinth with an impromptu roof over it, sometimes containing hundreds of tiny stores. From what I saw, employees at these shops tend to be women.

It would hard for me to describe what impressed me the most in Ukraine, although if I had to pick, it would be women. Their quiet dignity through hardships that most of us in the West will never know is surpassed only by their ability to deal with them.

Just like anywhere in the world, the rich never count when trying to understand a country. Anywhere in the wealthy areas of Ukraine, barring the fact that there's little English and practically nobody is black, yellow, red or brown, one of their shopping malls could easily fit anywhere on the East Coast, north of the palm trees. All the brands are here, from the fancy drinks prized because they are French or American, everything with English is valued as being better- all of this is here. This is the slice of life that you get when you look at the wealthy anywhere; somehow, it always transforms itself to wanting to be in Paris or London, maybe the south of something Mediterranean. The expensive jars of olives with a festive, nonchalant logo that's made to look old and rustic, yes, those too are easily found.

What I just mentioned matters as the average salary in the oblast I find myself in, this word translates to roughly a province or a state, is something around the figure of 141 Canadian dollars, per month. Minimum wage, as it stands for the Ukraine in general, is something like half of this. That four-dollar Borsch, their national soup of sorts, that came with a chicken wrap? If lucky, this is something a young couple would treat themselves to every couple of weeks. My point: money is rare.

Yet with women, it's hard to know if there is poverty, even from a Ukrainian standard. They are impeccable, as a hard guideline; they are always pretty, they are always neat, well dressed, and purposeful. They are dotting mothers, loving grandmothers and their families are lucky to have them. They are the ones who walk their children to school, tend to their families as best they can and make this country survive. I have no idea if it would be of use to comment on some of the men in this country, many with their fat stomachs or emaciated, alcoholic selves, lounging around their antiquated taxis and trying to charge some rare tourist ten times what a cab fare is worth. Have you not figured out that if nobody is in your cab, you will make no money instead of at least the going rate? What I just said is by no means commentary on all men, or most men: what I am telling you is that virtually no woman in this country would act in such way.

For the average woman in this country, there is a real way to differentiate between those who have just a bit of money and those who have none. As appearance to them is their way of showing the world that they are neither unsuccessful nor a pity case, their dress is always what they can afford. There is but one thing here that demonstrates the difference between the average, which is poor, and the below average, which is nearly abject.

The magic ingredient is makeup.

I'm not implying that women are dolled up to the point that they look like China dolls. That said, imagine a tasteful amount of powder, a little lipstick, and some eyeliner: this goes a long way to exemplify what is already a typically beautiful, Ukrainian woman. All they do is but accent what they already have, and this is the best way for them to, as a paradox, hide how they are really feeling, what would be unthinkable to show to the rest of the world.

If you look closely, those who cannot afford products stick out. The dark, tired eyes and those symmetrical, red stripes that people get under their orbits are present. So far, this tell has been the only difference, between seeing who belongs to the poor versus those condemned to the abject. As they walk, their clothing is just as clean, just as well scrubbed and well presented, there is no difference really in how they talk to others and walk; what you see is what they are unable to hide, as they lack that monetary reality to mask it.

In the poorer malls, in the less wealthy areas, I sat in a coffee shop that had particle board as walls with a poster stamped on it that showed what they can sell you; there were four cakes in a display case that could fit fifty. I suspect they have been there, unsold, for a very long time. As I watched Ukrainian women walk their children, their grandmothers, as they carried their bags of vegetables or a paper package with butcher meat, the obvious became even more glaring.

The stripes, more stripes, endless, endless stripes.

UNIVERSITY

Were you to take a walk in any neighbourhood in Lviv, one of the few guarantees I can give is that you will not see much in the way of ethnic diversity. Unless you're Slavic (or white, they can't really tell the difference), there's no way you can blend in. One of the biggest differences you first notice, from a Canadian perspective at least, is that Ukraine consists of essentially homogenous looking people. Put another way: immigration isn't a common thing.

Yet, you would eventually stumble into a neighborhood where Black students, speaking seemingly fluent Ukrainian, are common. This took me a while, to have such an observation, and my initial assumption is that there was some glaring diversity I had missed. Odd I thought, I've been here for months, so why am seeing this for the first time?

The shorthand reply is that I didn't miss anything in terms of longstanding communities: these students, almost all from Africa, come to Ukraine for the quality of their universities. Far less expensive that those you find in the European Union, with visa entry requirements that are more accessible, these students come to Ukraine to study (generally) medicine or engineering. Before they do so, they're enrolled in intensive Ukrainian for several months, and, based on what interpreters would tell me, one can have an adequate grasp of the language in a matter of four months.

The impeccable interior of Lviv Polytechnic National University.

The future of Ukraine, in the positive sense, will be determined and shown through its universities. I was moved, deeply so, by the efforts Ukraine puts towards educating their youth. This is not a freebie, nor is it anything like what we North Americans understand university to be. It is, for many, their redemption, and a rare chance at betterment. They know that they will have one chance, and one alone, regarding their studies. Failure, with regards to performance and success in a program is just not within their options. I make no illusions: the vast majority don't even consider the option of failure. Here's why.

Out of what we could try to help Ukrainians with, we have nothing to teach them when it comes to how students should behave. Clean and pressed clothes, books that are neither drawn in nor damaged, learners that shuffle quietly into classrooms, through their vast, impressive faculties that are well maintained and free of clutter. There are very few adds or frosh celebrations; in fact, the idea that somehow their four years is clouded by alcohol or parties is simply foreign to them.

They work, and they work hard. So valued are their studies that if you have the best grades of your class, one typical reward is to issue the rough salary that you would receive in your chosen profession, before you've even graduated; students that arrive second and third get incentives as well. They will work, and study, and work some more. The luckier ones will dedicate themselves entirely to acquiring knowledge, while the majority will find work somewhere to supplement their needs for a basic lodging.

To me, it brought the discipline (I use this word very liberally) we see in Canadian universities to shame. How many times when I was studying part-time did one of my peers spend most of his days drinking, having sex or simply not doing what, if I remember correctly, is the point of higher learning. The extravagance or, should I say, excess so often seen in Canada is simply not present. A lack of choice, no doubt, still, the idea of their work ethic and dedication to their studies was a truly humbling experience.

Unlike many countries that are facing severe difficulty, I was impressed to find out that there is no intention to transform schools of higher learning into institutions that teach in English. No, in Ukraine we speak, read, and are taught in Ukrainian. In contrast, how many countries have I seen that have had the misguided belief that if we only just switch to English and Americanize ourselves everything will be all right; they have no such ambitions here. As for the foreign students, and there are many, it is common for them to hire a tutor so that they can learn basic Ukrainian before they attend university. The quality of their schools, all things considered, is very high. Medical facilities and engineering here, remove the fact that they operate with equipment and facilities from forty years ago, are easily compatible with what you could expect from the West.

There are very few advertisements for cellphones, beauty products or the latest whatever. With a few exceptions in their hallways or at the entrances for student associations, their universities are exactly what they are supposed to be: a pillar of knowledge and a testament to what they can offer the next generation.

I notice that this is one of the few places where no-one (or virtually so) is even noticing me. They are simply too busy quietly going to their next lecture, with small, pliable document holders that contain their latest assignments. They go by you with almost no pause whatsoever.

The results of such discipline are telling. I was in a southern village near the Moldovan border when I met with a Canadian Physicians Assistant (basically, a highly trained nurse that can prescribe medications and even diagnose certain illnesses). Asking him what he thought of the medical facilities of Ukraine, as in, could they be comparable to those one could find in Canada, without much of a pause he said that, remove money, we would probably be just like them. Their doctors, so he was telling me, if given a few months to learn how to navigate modern medical equipment, would easily be employable in any Canadian hospital. How about something like surgery I asked, could it be done it Ukraine? The reply was simple: it could be done (and well), except that it would be with equipment several decades older than ours. The end results would be essentially the same as what we would find in Canada.

With modest economic abilities, limited resources, and the lack of vast international agreements that we have in Canada, that Ukraine performs as well as it does is a testament to their discipline in academia. This explains why, walking in certain neighborhoods in downtown Lviv, it takes no time to see diversity not seen in most of Ukraine; international students come here to become doctors, scientists, engineers. A high-quality education system, combined with visa standards that are lower than most places in Europe, results in a rarely observed degree of the passing of life-saving knowledge.

This brings me to something of Ukrainian minds, what appears as typical. From my standpoint, at least with Ukrainians around my age, they come off as somewhat robotic. Point A to point B, one task at a time, to which you fully dedicate yourself. Be they checking your flight status on a monitor or serving you at a restaurant, to use a metaphor, it looks to the common observer that they are curing cancer; their level of focus is that high. Everything is done purposefully, with implication.

As I was leaving one of their faculties,

you could see high school students being guided through the halls by a university undergraduate. You want to come here? Make a better life for yourself and your family, have a chance to advance past what your parents are doing? Here are the rules: we take the most serious of students with the best grades, and we offer no chance to those who are not implicated, fully, to their studies.

Like most things in this country, they are told the rules once, and few expect a second explanation. As I watched the students hear what the undergraduate was telling them, their reaction was quiet, total attention. Like many concepts and values here, the advice given was quick and simply, the rest of the work is up to them.

TATIANA

I've always found it more difficult to find the perspective of a woman. Maybe it's because I'm a man, maybe because women are not in positions of power in most parts of the world- I don't know. For Ukraine, their reality is somewhat different: from all the women I talked to, Tatiana was by far the most interesting, honest, and matter of fact.

To be fair, Tatiana and I met probably around a hundred times, in some instances I would have up to fifteen minutes to talk to her; our relationship, if I can call it as such, took months to build. What first started as a polite excuse for me to practice my abhorrent Ukrainian, and her with English that was far better than what she pretended it to be, we got along well without any intentions from one another.

Women will tell you things about men that you would otherwise never know. As I know I've made clear by now, the level of pride men possess in Ukraine is so high that I don't think I could have an honest conversation about weakness. However, if you take your time and build relationships based on trust and mutual respect, women may yield more information than a man ever would. In but a sentence, women generally don't build a small world around them that's constructed of pride, bravado, and ego.

Like virtually all women in Ukraine, Tatiana was at least beautiful. Her clear, piercing blue eyes, vanilla skin and impeccable dress had a dignity and class that isn't the norm in Canada. Measured and polite when she spoke, she was ethnically Russian and had spent most of her life in Western Ukraine, working in the service industry. Bilingual by birth, she self taught herself English, Polish, and was working on German.

I think the reason why her and I got along so well is because respect is a universal theme. The reputation Canadians have is envied: Americans often pretend to be one of us when they travel: they have a sad reputation of thinking they are better than others and are perceived, often, as self-entitled. No matter the country, I still cringe when I see the stereotypically overweight, loud American bellowing for a Coors Light, football jersey and baseball cap included, all the while appearing shocked that not everyone speaks English. That I have never been confused as an American is likely a testament to the very Canadian values of respect, humility, and the strict understanding that I am owed nothing special in a country that has its own values. I wear it as a badge of honour.

I still remember the first day we met. I was asking for something in Ukrainian that was probably so poorly pronounced that it was undecipherable, to which Tatiana then looks at me slightly puzzled. I apologize, try again, and after my second attempt, she smirks and says something along the lines of "if I had to guess, you would probably be British, but probably Canadian." I nodded, we both laughed, and our curious relationship of sorts started that day.

It began with a joke, one that I'm told is very Russian.

Alex, said Tatiana, what did the turd say to the orange?

I have no idea, what did he say?[20]

Oh orange, I envy you. For you are an orange, and I am a turd. Unlike you, I am useless.

The orange replied to the turd.

Do not worry, o turd, for one day, I shall be just like you. I too shall become useless.

That's the joke. That's it.

There I am, looking confused, while she's giggling after saying the orange is going to someday be as useless as the poop. The punchline is that one day we're all going to die, and ultimately life is a bad joke. In the end, everything is useless. I tell this joke in that, while Tatiana and I became friends of sorts, we come from very different backgrounds and our senses of humour, if I can call it so, differ wildly!

Over more than a few coffees, Tatiana explained to me how it was to grow up in Ukraine; what matters to most families, and cultural norms that, while not foreign to me, were certainly more direct.

To begin with, she explained to me the special role grandmothers have in Ukraine.[21]

Women live far longer in this part of the world than men, and this is mainly due to lifestyle choices. While smoking may have diminished, it would be fair to say that a large segment of Ukrainian men are addicted for life. Combined with a love of alcohol that would surely be a central, national vice, what results is a life expectancy, according to 2013 data, of about 66 years for men. In contrast, women live at least ten years longer.

For most children, memories of their grandfathers are generally shorter and nearly nostalgic, made with what little they remember about them. By the time children reach their teens, most of them no longer have a living grandfather, yet their grandmother remains. Typically, she will be healthy, very cognisant and will be almost exclusively dedicated to her family's well-being.

That this reality is due, at least in part, to lifestyle choices of men, the conclusion is that grandmothers play a central role of bridging generational differences. Typically, they broker the expectations of parents with the reality of what their children are going through.

For example, Tatiana is working in the service industry in a world full of men: they may not have the best of intentions towards her. This fact is not really known to her parents, yet her grandmother, on the other hand, is far more aware of her daily life.

When her parents start to question Tatiana's day, generally her grandmother will carefully steer the conversation from questions that are too direct or simply unattractive. She will cover for Tatiana when she works an overtime shift in a dubious social setting, will offer insight on how her father is doing (as the dad wouldn't want to worry his daughter). In short, I don't know if Ukraine is fundamentally a matriarchy, however, the role that grandmothers play reminded me of a maestro conducting different musical instruments.

She is also the collective memory of her family. For those of working age, life in Ukraine demands extremely long hours and they often don't have the time to properly interact with one another. For the grandmother, though, she knows her grandchildren often better than their parents do and will keep everyone in tune with what's going on.

The grandmother will be less judgemental. For the father, like most on earth, he will be protective of his daughter beyond realism and expects behaviour that's outdated. The grandmother, on the other hand, will be less critical, judgemental, or moralistic. She will listen, offer limited advice; her point is unqualified care.

And women in general, I ask, what's something that's important, or expected?

Tatiana tells me that while men have a clear need to be dressed well, for women this is even more true. In any large city in Ukraine, she said, you wouldn't see much difference in how women dress when they go to work, to a picnic, or to school. In many ways, there is no "lesser" dress code; they are always impeccable. She tells me that if she wore a necklace that her friends thought looked stupid, she would never wear it again.

Yet, one of the most interesting concepts we discussed was her view of how someone born in Ukraine will think, versus somebody born in Russia. In the end, while they are similar, the difference lies in how they react to others, and the public display of emotion plays out. So:

I offered an extreme hypothetical as to parse the difference between what would happen in Moscow versus Kyiv. When I say extreme, I mean for these parts of the word: what I'm going to describe can be seen in any major metropolitan city in the West, and nobody would blink an eye at this (I think?) or, at minimum, this act would be perfectly acceptable.[22]

Two men in their late fifties, holdings hands, and going for a walk. They are obviously gay; they both appear effeminate. In Moscow they walk at the Red Square, in Kyiv at Glory Park. Both sites, relative to each country, would be of comparable importance.

Tatiana is a product of her upbringing. Homosexuality is not viewed by her as a sin nor as a degenerate lifestyle for the sick: she's far more elevated in her way of thinking. However, Tatiana views this sort of sexual behaviour as odd, difficult to understand (in that its generally perceived as a choice) and she would not want to see this in a family member. Her view is that someone with homosexual tendencies would be in for a hard life; she would rather not see someone she cares about suffer.

In Moscow, the idea of two men holding hands in public area, compounded with the obviousness of them being gay is, to start with, completely unacceptable. It wouldn't happen, she said, and even if it did, that would not last long.

What would happen, I asked.

People would at first look at them as if they're the devil incarnate, and traditionally stoic people would look at them as if they had the plague. It would not take long for younger men, those that are already xenophobic, to see what's going on and, on the balance of probabilities, both gay men would be beaten nearly to death. The police would be called (maybe), and their disgust would be hidden. It would be unlikely that anyone would be arrested, as the generalized view from some Russians is that these two gay men got exactly what they deserved.

Okay, now tell me about Kyiv.

In Kyiv, it may be that some people think the same way as they would in Moscow. They might think that they're the devil incarnate, mentality ill, degenerates, and the like. They might even glance at them with mild signs of disgust (and it would be mild). The difference though is that it would be surprising that anything would happen to them. To have young men beat them, unless said men were drunk, is unlikely.

This is what I'm getting at in terms of understanding the difference. Ukrainians (to include those ethnically Russian) are far more careful about what they say and do in public, versus those from the Russian Federation. They carefully measure their statements in public, even more so in front of people they do not know and are good at hiding their thoughts from others. They are not aggressive in a way that you would see in Russia; I would think that they are more suspicious of others than their cousins to the east, and view assertiveness by violence as a last resort, not the first.

I would see this kind of behaviour throughout their country. Ask a question that might have some controversy or debate? A typical reaction is that the person you're talking to responds by first asking your opinion and will build on whatever you just said. Don't see this as weakness: it's their cautious nature that wants to gauge who and what you are first, then maybe add to it by conveying a curated viewpoint. If they don't know you, why would they trust you by conveying an opinion that might get them in trouble?

Whereas in Russia, you will not have that measure of pause. In Canada, an expression that's used to describe the scaling of violent interaction is known as playing "pokey chest." Basically, imagine two men yelling at each other with one of them eventually poking his finger into the others chest, the yelling increasing, and the other man eventually poking his rival's chest in turn. As this goes on, the chest poking might stop, and fists, while rare, might start to come out.

If you were to play this game in Russia, and I've asked this question many times in Ukraine, the shorthand reply is that you better be willing to go to war with whomever you're doing this with. The Russian will not stop, he can't. The calm, calculating demeanour you see in Ukraine, one that tries to deal with things in a more subtle way is not a luxury that the average Russian, within their federation, would be able to afford.

We went much further into our conversations,and it led into obligations that men have towards women. I remember how it started: as we were chatting after I had lunch, I noticed an older couple that was coming to the hotel. The man, at least in his fifties, exited his at least fifteen-year-old car, walked to the passenger side, and opened the door for his wife. He opened an umbrella for her, walked by her in the rain, and opened the door. He then took his hat off, took her coat, and went about finding a coat check for them while she relaxed in a comfy chair. This might seem old fashioned to us, although I guarantee you this is the norm in Ukraine.[23]

Looking at this benign scene, I commented that this man is gentleman, and Tatiana genuinely had no idea what I was talking about. The car door, the umbrella, the hat, these things are so basic that to her, they didn't even warrant a second thought. When she asked me if this was uncommon in Canada, I gave a polite non-answer (I didn't want to come off as a savage), and it was clear that gender roles are more defined in Ukraine, which I'd argue doesn't necessarily make them sexist.

What's the worst thing a Ukrainian man could do?

Well, if you get your girlfriend pregnant and you're already married, that's not good. Not a deal breaker though, at least in the eyes of your parents. They won't disown you for that, although if you're savage enough not to take care of her and that baby, you're done. As in, your father won't talk to you again and you're on your own, totally cut of from your family.

Hmm, interesting.

Speaking of marriage, what about a foreigner marrying a Ukrainian (woman)? Would she be perceived as finding a way to get out of Ukraine?

Pause.

That's uncommon, she probably wouldn't accept unless she knew that her parents would be taken care of, and she'd prefer it if her family came with her. She wouldn't just leave, that would be like abandoning her own.

Okay.

Now this is from the perspective of someone that has a good family. The undertone of how women are treated in some areas, or the underbelly of what you see in Kyiv, is a totally different matter. Here's the sideline.

I want you to imagine an old, overweight man, someone that hasn't seen the inside of a gym in at least thirty years. Bad skin, yellowed teeth, and whatever mental picture you can make of a dirty, middle-aged man is what I'd like you to visualize. Someone with baggy clothes, slouches a bit when he walks, standing in the middle of a large public square holding a brightly coloured flower. There he stands, with a creepy smile, just looking into space, holding his flower. For a moment, you might think that he's mentally challenged, although he comes off as just a little too purposeful for that kind of thing.

Then, a towering bear of a man, someone that looks like he could be a heavyweight boxer, in a sleek black leather jacket and fists the size of casaba melons walks right up to him. The middle-aged man nods, smiles even more, and the stoicism of the giant concludes to looking behind him, nodding, and then a third person comes their way.

See, for me, when she's wearing six-inch heels, a skirt that couldn't possibly be be four inches shorter, and it looks like she put on makeup with a patching trowel, all of this in the dead of winter, that's a sign. I'm going with the idea that she's neither a geologist nor a city counsellor, and the middle-aged man, just oozing of scummy, hands her the flower. She then hands it to the large gorilla, who in turn walks away, as they head off to one of the various extraordinarily expensive downtown hotels. Yes, I know this happens in any city, although Ukraine has the unenviable reputation as a haven for prostitution and sex trafficking.

UKRAINIAN BUREAUCRACY…

Tired and having learned that Ukrainian bureaucracy is not akin to logic, reason, or common sense, I arrived at the airport at least three and a half hours early. Maybe, so I thought, more time will be needed to get through the airport than most that I've been to; if I've learned anything since arriving in country, all mighty process will win over my need to get on an plane.

Ticket and passport says the check-in lady.

I give her a print-out, one that she seems to be studying as if it can cure cancer. After what felt like two minutes, she starts to input something in her computer, glancing at me now and then, studying my e-ticket several times.

Where are you going?

Canada.

Do you have any luggage?

I wanted to be sarcastic. I didn't say this, but I really wanted to. Luggage? Of course not: I didn't bring any with me, I've worn the same thing for months on end and I don't believe in showering, removing the cost of expensive toiletries. Yeah, the luggage you clearly saw me carry to your booth is just for my health, no need to bring it with me or anything.

Yes miss, I have luggage.

Do you have your luggage form?

Luggage form?

Why (nearly a gasp!), you must have your luggage form! This is a required form! Needed to process your luggage!

Uh, well, okay, can I just drop my luggage off here, and you can just give me my luggage form?

(Her reaction: as if I told her that I'm going to wax my car with her wedding dress.)

I cannot do such a thing! You must go to the luggage center to process this demand! Return once you have the luggage form! Take this form that authorizes you to check in your luggage!

I head off to another counter, conveniently nowhere near hers.

Another lady looks at me. Yes hi, I'd need to

check in my luggage. Here's my e-ticket, passport, and the form that this lady gave me to give to you so I can check in my things.

Just like lady number one, she studies my forms as if they have the solution to cure cancer. Then, after a couple of minutes, she types something on her computer that has to do with my passport, e-ticket, and the form I was just given. This takes at least twenty minutes.

Where are you going?

Canada.

Oh, this requires additional authorization since you are travelling internationally. I need to get this authorization before I can process your luggage.

I mean, the lady at the other counter told me to come to see you to check in luggage.

Yes, but the form is for non-international travel! I will fix this with authorization!

I can't make this up: after what had to be at least three different phone calls, a pilot came to the luggage both. There they are, scrutinizing my documents and glancing at me periodically, all the while talking in low voices as if this is something complex and/or mysterious. Another ten minutes later, they take my luggage, stamp the form the counter lady gave me, and give me another form, stapled to the first, that are both required for me to get my plane ticket.

So I walk back to the first booth and I now have my e-ticket, passport, form number one, stamped, form number two, unstamped, and a receipt for my luggage; all of this, I'm told, is absolutely required in order to continue my check-in.

I get back in line (and of course, it's busy), wait another twenty minutes, and face a new counter number one lady.

Ticket and passport.

Hi, I just got back from the luggage counter and –

TICKET AND PASSPORT.

I put all five documents on her counter. Immediately, she looks at me as if I'm mentally challenged until I remove everything except for my ticket and passport.

Where are you going?

Canada (sigh).

Do you have any luggage?

Yes.

Do you have your luggage form?

(I give her both).

She studies them as if they have the cure for, you guessed it.

Wait, she says, they checked you in with a domestic travel form!

I don't know what to tell you.

We can't process this! You need a different form!

I mean the pilot (as I look over, there he was, I waived), yeah him! He said it was ok!

The pilot nods and says something, she looks at me, stoic, no reaction at all. Eventually, she hands me my ticket.

Very well. You have completed this segment of checking in. Proceed to customs. She stamps the second form and gives me a third.

Let's count: passport, e-ticket, luggage form of some kind number one, luggage form of some kind number two, receipt, and third form from the counter that doesn't have the required stamp. I'm up to six documents, all of them required, as I shuffle to the customs office, wondering what tower of babel, soviet-form-worshipping-process is about to come my way.

The frustration that I'm hopefully conveying is one of those remnants from a soviet era, one that worships extremely stupid process for the sake of having one. In the end, as I'm waiting by the airport terminal, I had nine forms.

This isn't unique to airports though; there is a very linear way of looking at process in Ukraine. Normally, talking about bureaucracy is about as interesting as watching paint dry, though looking back, it comes off as nearly absurd in virtually everything that involves money or authority.

A restaurant menu? Why, this requires a stamp! As to attest to the validity and authenticity of said menu!

Hotel receipt? Stamp!

Laundry that you had washed, returned with an inventory of duly submitted items?

Stamp! Stamp! Stamp!

And God help you if you don't have your stamp; why, this would mean that an authority of some kind has not certified the purchase, sale, or ownership of items! Really though, I mean, isn't a credit card statement showing that I stayed at the hotel indicative enough of purchase?

That blank state I mentioned earlier when I asked if I could just get the luggage form from the counter lady? Yeah, that's the same look you get from pretty much everyone if you dare question the stamps.

All that to say that they love their mighty, mighty stamps.

Yet it doesn't end there. This is something that's fascinating to me, in that what is patently known to be true somehow needs be repeated. I mean, Ukrainians aren't stupid, far from it, yet there's this seeming obsession with stating the obvious.

What a helpful, highly insightful sign. Without it, I'm sure that everyone would think its okay to rip toilets out from the concrete flooring, carrying them on their backs.

When I was in Kyiv, public facilities, to include subways, are at least as clean as what you would find in Montreal or Toronto. Built under communist control, most public transportation is very lavish, and the subway system that you find in Kyiv is one of the deepest in the world, due to the bygone possibility of a nuclear strike. The same can be said of clear streets, well scrubbed cafés, and general pride in objects that people have. It feels like Europe, as it is part of it, and the efficiency and cleanliness is, all things considered, top notch.

Yet, you have signs to inform you of things not to do, just like this one. Again: Ukrainians aren't stupid; it's just that there's this intangible, love of administrative bureaucracy that makes no sense. Combined with stating the patently obvious, as in, what doesn't need to be told, the result in something that I've never seen anywhere else. On one hand I have people that are exceedingly disciplined with studies, work, and family. On the other, I have this odd state apparatus that seems to think that they're the dumbest people that have ever walked the earth. Soviet legacy? Maybe a bureaucracy that's, assumingly, totally disconnected? Make work projects for the civil service? You tell me.

THE CHURCH

Roughly fifteen years ago, mental health evolved into something else than a stigma for Canadian men. Being part of the first group of millennials, from my teenage years I remember very well that depression was generally seen as a moral failing, that therapy was for weaklings, and any mental health issue, especially one that a man struggled with, was solely due to their own failures. In plain English, if you were caught going to a mental health clinic, while serving in the military or law enforcement, you could be certain that your career would be over. I'm sure that it wasn't much better for most men that didn't wear a uniform, prior to entering the 21st; it might have just been easier for them to hide their pain.

And hiding pain is what men do. From generations before me, the main solution most men would find tended to be at the bottom of a bottle, never actually there, their quest for solution surmised in going from one drink to the next. From what I'm told by those who are older than me (read: the most honest of their generations), booze never worked. At best, it might numb pain until your liver and a bad night of sleep gives you reprieve, and that's about it. Many men, some far stronger than me, would lose themselves in alcohol as it appears to be one of the few (if not the only) coping mechanisms that was socially acceptable.

Ukraine being in many ways a time machine to me, their mentality is one or two generations removed from mine.[24] A therapist? Psychology? In but a word, unthinkable. Mental health would require an opening of a new concept of wellness, and that day, while it may come to Ukraine, will certainly not be the norm within my lifetime.

And they do have hard lives; they do need to have a socially acceptable form of release. As alcohol is just about the only one available, it is, I'm certain, "the" vice that permeates Ukraine. How else can one cope? How else can someone get through working twelve-hour days, six days a week, for a meagre paycheck, a state that struggles to provide essentials, and a downward spiral that's not seeing an end, at least anytime soon?

This is the average man, the one that isn't fighting in the eastern part of his country. From a military or security perspective, imagine what you would look like if you spent a solid year in a trench, urinating in a bucket, eating rotten produce and having a lifestyle comparable to what you could read as representative of the First World War? How could anyone maintain mental health for a sustained period in such conditions? When these men return home, often they go from not having a shower for weeks on end to being in their living room, with their kids, within 48 hours. There is no way, in my opinion, that there won't be difficulties in adjusting.

Earlier, I talked about how weakness is never rewarded in Ukraine, how having somebody know that you aren't doing well, with maybe the exception of the closest family members (and even then...) is cultural anathema. For all the understandable reasons, that's just the way it is.

This is when the church comes into play.

Catholicism[25] offers a sacred bond of trust between the priest and the penitent. If someone is truly in pain based on their experiences, what they have done and/or what's been done to them, Catholic beliefs allow for a man to confess and talk about it to another human being- one that's dedicated his life to an understanding of right and wrong. In exchange for the man trusting the priest, what he receives is a pastoral tradition, one that transcends dozens of generations, that offers a conduit towards improved mental health. I am not suggesting that pastoral care is synonymous (or even comparable) to what mental health professional can offer; what I am saying is that it does great good.

Priests in Ukraine are likely the largest repository of secrets that will never be told. Catholic tradition makes it clear: whatever the penitent tells the priest, within the right of confessional, can never be mentioned to another. Period. This means that in a country where weakness is never rewarded, here is one of the extraordinarily rare instances where a Ukrainian can deal with issues that disturb him greatly, without the fear of consequence that comes with trusting another.

Post Traumatic Stress, biploar disorder, depression, all of these clinical terms are not well known, much less accepted, in this part of the world. Yet, pastoral animation does offer a measure of peace, identity, and belief in that things get better. From the perspective of many locals, both civilian and military, the church offers what little they have when it comes to mental health, and I believe that their faith is effective in helping them deal with their lives.

Out of respect, this will be the only time where I won't talk about a specific person that I met, sharing their viewpoint; I will not discuss even the passing conversations I've had with religious officials (who never told me specifics towards any of their cases), nor the opinion of locals towards the good that religion does for them. I find this too personal, delicate, and something I'm not comfortable sharing.

Returning to the church in general, if someone were to simply pass-through Ukraine or visit their country for a week, one could easily think that they're deeply religious. In truth, this is an overly simplistic way of looking at the relationship Ukraine has to religion, in that it encompasses social services, the most comparable service we would identify as counselling, and respect for their history and traditions. Although this might seem contradictory, their respect for religious institutions, I'd argue, are not generally because of a belief in God per se. Rather, it is a belief in their community.

I'll reintroduce my grandfather for a moment. In Quebec, prior to the 1960's, a village church was the physical representation of community. No matter the degree of poverty in rural Quebec (and in general, these communities were very, very poor), to use my grandfather's viewpoint, they still built what looks like a castle in the name of collective good. In that way, churches in Ukraine, be they Catholic or Orthodox, are identical in what they represent. I doubt very much that there is any coercion on the part of villagers to contribute to their beauty; the pride they have in them is tremendous.

This is where what little they have can be shared with those who have even less. This is where community events generally happen, where they pay respect to the war dead, where big life events occur. It is the same building generations before them frequented, and it is a link to the past.

It's also one of the few institutions, I'd argue, that isn't viewed as totally corrupt. From the era of the communists, or if we go even further during the time of the tzars, there these buildings were essentially offering the same services as they now do. They offer a reminder of their struggles: everywhere throughout Ukraine you can see churches that have bullet holes in them from the Second World War, that are kept as is to remind of times more difficult.

These institutions have their place cemented in Ukraine; I can't imagine them leaving. Out of a respect for tradition, knowledge of what works for them, there are no organizations worth mentioning that could replace religion, or the benefits of a community based on the latter.

IN CLOSING

Over two centuries ago, the United States invaded Canada with the firm intention of annexing it into their republic. To most American minds at that time, to include then former President Thomas Jefferson, the view was that Canada could be conquered and integrated into the United States within a few weeks, ridding, according to them, any trace of the Crown within North America. We now call this event the War of 1812.

Back then, even though North America was considered by colonial powers as the backwater of Europe, it stood that American forces were vastly superior to those Canadian. I will skirt over the ideology except to say that American mentalities held then (and maybe still now?) a nearly infectious love of individual choice, revolutionary ideals of democracy, and the like. I'd go so far as to mention that, in many of their military units, it was the soldiers that would elect their officers, on the basis that the proper way to command is somehow synonymous with being popular.

From the perspective of the United States,

there was no doubt that a far smaller group, one that believed in loyalty to the Crown, would collapse almost immediately when invaded. More irrelevant still, by their own words, was the presence of a now dated French colony that, so they thought, would have no issue with yet another regime. Combined with a total disregard to First Nations influence, one that massively turned the tides of war, American self-confidence bloated along as they invaded Canadian soil. This invasion would mark the first time the United States, as a sovereign nation, had declared war.

Two years later, American forces had been pushed back to such an extent that their capital, the same that stands today, was completely ransacked by their supposedly weakly, northern neighbour. One of the legacies of this war is still visible: if you've ever wondered why someone chose to paint the White House white, that's because it was the only colour they had left. Other destroyed buildings included the United States Treasury, the Capitol (so that includes the Library of Congress, Supreme Court, Congress itself) and, in short, not much of value remained.

As they were fleeing the capital, indeed running for their lives, I wonder what American leaders were thinking. President James Madison was in office and I'm certain that, no matter what was going through his mind, he must have asked himself how this could have happened. During his exodus to Maryland, he surely wondered how an irrelevant military force was now ransacking the United States. Not only defeated to the tune of thousands of war dead inside Canada: the tides had turned with disastrous results within their own country.

The reasons for this reversal, and I'd say utter embarrassment for the Americans, are varied. While Canada and the U.S are now great allies, the War of 1812 is taught very differently in either nation. From my side, so to speak, the essential reason why the United States lost (or at least, did not win) was a belief in the weakness of its opponent and the idea that size equals victory. Stated differently, there appeared to be a view that due to their size, their opponent wouldn't (or couldn't) stand a chance.

In using this to talk about Ukraine, I think the parallel is clear.

To make an exception and allow myself to be the typical Canadian, I'll say this politely: Ukraine has been through more difficulties than most nations could imagine. Were I to take Europe, geographically speaking, I think most people would be hard pressed to find a state that has had to endure more suffering than Ukraine has, and at that, for a period of something like 80 years. Of all the countries that I have visited, worked, or transited through I have rarely, if ever, seen so much pain that is largely no fault of their own.

To think that the recent events in the eastern

part of Ukraine will somehow prevent them from maintaining and/or defending their sovereignty is patently absurd, and I would argue utterly foolish on the part of the Russian Federation. While I have tried through these pages to emphasize, and then emphasize the emphasis that Russian people are not their government, I'm fully aware that no matter what I say, I will be misquoted and misinterpreted. I will state this once more: I greatly respect Russians as a people and believe that what their government is doing is not in the best interest of its citizens.

To the government of the Russian Federation, I'd suggest a moment of pause. If generations of control, either directly or by puppet, did not quash Ukrainian identity, language, or beliefs, I would suggest that this might be a hint that they will never go away. If mass starvations, war, forceful annexation, criminalizing opinions, censoring identities, bribing their officials (the list could be hundreds of pages long) has not diminished the resolve of Ukrainians, there is a lesson to be learned.

I realize that the Russian Federation is likely nostalgic of the power it held thirty years ago; it isn't happy that nearly all its former satellites prefer the West. From their point of view, I understand that Ukraine being a member state of NATO puts the West at your doorstep, and this is an unthinkable outcome. The solution, so it seems, is to continue a low intensity war on their border with Ukraine, thus ensuring that NATO won't allow a country at war to join its ranks, or for that matter the European Union. It makes sense, it's a logical step, and it is, above all else, putrid in its amoral pragmatism.

I would invite the reader to observe the voluminous instances where this hasn't worked. Barring the epic fails of nations trying to dominate Afghanistan, smaller, determined countries, so long as they never give up, tend to win over occupiers. The British Empire failed against Ireland, Finland was never under control of the USSR, China did not win when invading Vietnam. There are no shortages of such examples, and looking towards Ukraine, I see no reason to think that the conclusions will be any different.

As I write this, the economy of the Russian Federation is in one of the poorest states it's been in since the fall of the Soviet Union. I need not throw many numbers and I think one example can do: for the average Russian male, you are eligible to obtain an old age pension, based on average life expectancy, a few years after you die. There are other priorities for the Russian Federation than to wage war in Ukraine, at the cost of providing a decent quality of life for its citizens.

While I don't usually place much time in offering predictions, my view is that this will be a long war. With the ATO now controlled by assorted criminal syndicates, the chaos that was made in this region, once hostilities are over, will take decades to repair. Many observers forget that the oblasts within the ATO, prior to Maidan, were some of the poorest within Ukraine; the result of years of conflict suggests that their current economic posture is terrible. As I write this, whatever economic viability once present has been scrapped beyond the reach of moderate solution.

Despite all of this, the fighting in the ATO is not the summum of Ukraine. One day, it too will prove to be no more than a chapter in their long, difficult history and remembered, I suspect, as a footnote compared to conflicts far more deadly.

Ukrainians are some of the most resilient and hardworking people that I have ever had the privilege to meet, and my aim was to explain how a nation with terrible odds has been able to overcome them. They are certainly imperfect: more stubborn than plow mules, proud above reason and not having yet learned, in general at least, that moderation tends to be key when drinking or smoking. Yet, those are small things in contrast to their overall character, values, and ethics.

Canada has over a million citizens that can trace their roots to Ukraine. About two years ago, I was driving through rural Manitoba, looking at the unlimited fields of wheat, interrupted by the occasional Canadian and Ukrainian flags. Looking at the people, whether they be in Canada or in Ukraine, there wouldn't be much of a difference. Family, good food, hard work. Canada would not be what it is without the input of generations of Ukrainians; they have greatly helped build a country like no other.

As I learned from driving throughout Ukraine, their flag is very much a map of how their country looks: blue is for the sky, yellow for their vast fields of wheat. I can see why Canada would be a good choice for Ukrainians, even more so the prairies.

Both nations share more in common versus what they don't, and my hope is that, looking forward, the steadfast commitment Canada has had towards Ukraine will neither falter nor diminish. As I said earlier, Canada has but a small dice to play on the international scene, and that we cast it in favour of Ukraine was the right thing to do. I have no doubt that, if roles were reversed, their dice would be cast for us.

ABOUT THE AUTHOR

Alexandre Fontaine

Alexandre Fontaine was part of the Government of Canada's assistance mission to Ukraine, having lived in country for over six months. During his 14 years at the Department of National Defence, he served in overseas deployments that include Afghanistan, Central America, and Eastern Europe. Holding degrees from Concordia University and the University of Manitoba, Alexandre is in the process of completing his Master of Liberal Arts at Harvard University, Division of Continuing Education (Extension School). This is his first book.

FOOTNOTES

[1] Incidentally enough, there is even less information on this famine. While we will never know for sure, there were at least 18 million dead. Other estimates place this number at 45 million.

[2] We often forget that the USSR and the Third Reich collaborated until Hitler decided to invade Russia. Monuments to World War Two, in Eastern Europe and Russia, usually identify 1941 to 1945 as the Great Patriotic War, conveniently leaving out what happened before Hitler and Stalin became enemies. Prior to Germany attacking the Soviet Union, Finland, Poland, Latvia, Lithuania, Estonia, and Romania (amongst others) were all invaded by the USSR. In almost all cases, these nations didn't regain their sovereignty for over 50 years.

[3] The one exception that I was told several times was for those who lived in the Carpathian Mountains. Apparently, that area speaks a dialect that is so, shall we say rustic, that even the average Ukrainian has a hard time understanding them. Due to its isolation, there was never much of an attempt to Russify them, though I digress.

[4] For the USSR to store enough nuclear material to level a continent within their borders, one can only imagine the control they had within Ukraine.

[5] This is a very relative term, one that I'm using to contrast Ukraine's difficulties circa 1991-2001. Better does not mean good.
[6] Since 2014, this part of Ukraine often referred to as the Anti-Terrorist Operation (ATO) Zone.
[7] I changed his name, as with all others. Also, I won't mention the name of the hotel because he might still work there.
[8] This is something I've seen through Ukraine, and it seems that this is a cultural thing.
[9] It is exceedingly rare that Ukrainians, at least in larger cities, can afford to live by themselves.
[10] I have no idea what's in this energy drink, except to tell you that two sips of it would wake up a coma induced horse. I've never seen it sold in North America and do yourself a favour, don't try it.
[11] It turns out that the reason why we believe in lawns (I found out afterwards) is due to the legacy of British propriety. It looks nice, it's a gloating piece and above all else, it has absolutely no purpose in life except to look good. Now I know.
[12] And God help you if you give someone a 500 Hryvna bill to pay for a box of saltines. Costing all of 20 Hryvna, she'll look at you as if to say "you've got to be kidding me" and will reward you with a giant wad of essentially worthless bills.
[13] I will never know if the logistics he speaks of will ever give him what he needs. For that matter, I don't think there's a way that he'd ever tell me.
[14] That's an actual response, produced and publicly endorsed by the Russian Federation. I can't make that up.

[15] True story: I've seen Ukrainian soldiers waiting in line in their underwear, for their only set of clothes to dry. They were in the drier.
[16] This is purely anecdotal.
[17] There are variants of this joke in about a half dozen other countries, ones that don't have the nicest of pasts with the Russian Federation.
[18] It's a talking fish.
[19] Finland gets an honourable mention, although it did relinquish some of its land after the Winter War.
[20] I have no idea if I should refer to poop as masculine or feminine.
[21] While she told me there's no way she'd know from personal experience, her view is that you would find a similar dynamic in Russia.
[22] This is one example of many.
[23] To be fair, this kind of behaviour is typical in Eastern Europe.
[24] In no way am I suggesting that Ukrainians are backwards or less evolved. Mental health is simply not a concept understood in general society, much like it was in Canada fifty years ago.
[25] I focus on the Catholic aspect as this was the faith tradition I was most exposed to in Ukraine. I have no doubt that orthodox liturgy has similar benefits to their parishioners.

REFERENCES AND SUGGESTED READINGS

The fundamental aim of what I wrote was to convey the lived experiences of individuals that, likely, wouldn't have had their voices heard otherwise (at least not in Canada). With that in mind though, the first few chapters discuss the socio-economic state of Ukraine and its history, so I'd be remiss if I didn't offer the reader the same resources that I had access to.

For information that refers to Euromaidan (to include some political background) or the Russian Federations interventions in Ukraine, I used both local and international sources. All of these are separate from my conversations with Ukrainians. Here are a few, all of them accessed no later than June 2021:

- BBC News. East Ukraine separatists seek union with Russia. https://www.bbc.com/news/world-europe-27369980 .

- Kyiv Post. EuroMaidan rallies in Ukraine – Nov. 21-23 coverage. https://www.kyivpost.com/article/content/euromaidan/euromaidan-rallies-in-ukraine-nov-21-23-coverage-332423.html?cn-reloaded=1
- Sputniknews. Ukraine must not blame neighbors for famine – Yanukovych. https://sptnkne.ws/kQge.
- The Guardian. Ukraine suspends talks on EU trade pact as Putin wins tug of war. https://www.theguardian.com/world/2013/nov/21/ukraine-suspends-preparations-eu-trade-pact

In terms of data and metrics, I used either information from the World Bank, United Nations or Ukrainian data from their statistics bureau:

- State Statistics Service of Ukraine (compendium, per year). http://www.ukrstat.gov.ua/operativ/operativ2007/ds/nas_rik/nas_e/nas_rik_e.html
- The World Bank (extensive, searchable data). https://data.worldbank.org/country/ukraine?view=chart
- United Nations Demographic Yearbook (2001). https://unstats.un.org/unsd/demographic/products/dyb/dybsets/2001%20DYB.pdf

I found the that following books were helpful for me to understand Ukraine. Most of them discuss the recent past, although I've included a few that focus on the twentieth century in general. For further readings on Ukraine, I'd suggest:

- Applebaum, Anne. Red Famine: Stalin's War on Ukraine. New York: Penguin Random House, 2017.
- Buttar, Prit. Retribution: The Soviet Reconquest of Central Ukraine, 1943. New York: Osprey Publishing, 2019.
- Galeotti, Mark. Armies of Russia's War in Ukraine. New York: Osprey Publishing, 2019.
- Plokhy, Serhii. The Gates of Europe: A History of Ukraine. New York: Perseus Books, 2015.
- Reid, Anna. Borderland: A Journey Through the History of Ukraine. London: Weidenfeld & Nicolson, 1997.
- Schlögel, Karl. Ukraine: A Nation on the Borderland. London: Reaktion Books, 2018.
- Subtelny, Orest. Ukraine: A History. Fourth Edition. Toronto: University of Toronto Press, 2009.
- Yekelchyk, Serhy. Ukraine: Birth of a Modern Nation. New York: Oxford University Press, 2007.

Manufactured by Amazon.ca
Bolton, ON

25187793R00083